INTRODUCTION

Which dead famous Queen Mary lost her head on Elizabeth I's chopping block?

BLOODY MARY

MARY QUEEN OF SCOTS

YOU'RE NOT EVEN IN THE RIGHT CENTURY!

MARY ANTOINETTE

ACTUALLY IT'S MARIE!

(Keen readers might notice a clue in the title of the book!)

GO AND GET YOUR OWN **DEAD FAMOUS** BOOKS!

SHOVE

JOSTLE

Mary started life at the top. She was queen of her own country at one week old, and queen twice over at 15 when her first hopeless husband became King of France. A year later he died, leaving the tall, beautiful and charming Scottish Queen on her ownsome. Read on and you can find out how the most desirable widow in Europe ended up going from one totally hopeless husband to another, and how they helped her down the road to ruin. (One was so awful that everyone else ganged up and murdered him and the other ended up raving mad, chained to a pillar...)

Mary's short reign in Scotland was packed with murders, battles, kidnappings and treason. Finally she fled her kingdom to England for protection ... or was it to try and grab the English crown? Her cousin, Queen Elizabeth I, 'protected' her for 19 years ... by keeping her in prison ... before chopping off her head.

Now you can check out what the Scots thought of their beautiful but troubled queen in the Scottish Herald, and what they plastered on the walls! Discover some Prickly Thistle Facts. Sneak a peek at Mary's letters from France to her mum back home in Scotland, and get the exclusive inside story when you read what Mary might have written in her secret diary.

INFANT QUEEN

Mary was born on 8 December 1542, in the middle of a war with England. Just six days later, her father, King James V, died, leaving the tiny baby Queen of Scots. The kingdom she inherited was a mess. It was dominated by powerful nobles who were split down the middle along religious lines. Some were Protestant, some Catholic. But probably the biggest problem that Scotland had to face was its powerful neighbour, England.

For centuries, war between England and Scotland had been more or less an annual fixture, basically because the kings of England wanted to take over Scotland. Sometimes they tried to be subtle about it and do it by marrying into the Scottish royal family. At other times they just sent troops up to Scotland to put the boot in. Sometimes they did both. Mary's grandad, James IV, was married to Henry VIII's sister, but that didn't stop Henry attacking Scotland, and as a result James IV was killed at the battle of Flodden in 1513.

The sudden death of Mary's granddad at Flodden meant that her dad became King of Scots when he was not yet two years old. It also meant that if his uncle Henry VIII (or his children) died without any legitimate heirs James (and his children) would have a very strong claim to the English throne ...

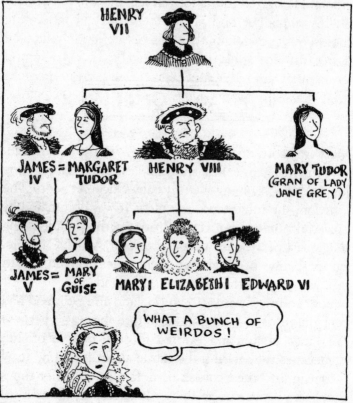

James V

While little James was growing up, Scotland was ruled by a regent – initially his mum, Margaret Tudor, with the help of pro-English nobles. Soon there was a struggle for power and the Scottish nobles chucked out Margaret and took control for ten years. Finally, when James was

13, Margaret's second husband, the Earl of Angus, took charge of the country – and of the young king, who was kept prisoner in Falkland Castle.

James escaped from Falkland aged 17, disguised as a groom. He started ruling for himself and was very tough on his stepfather and all his henchmen, confiscating their spoils and kicking them out of Scotland. In fact, he didn't trust any of his nobles. He liked to wander around the country dressed as a beggar or a servant, finding out what was really going on.

He was nicknamed the Gaberlunzie man (Gaberlunzie means tinker or traveller).

🌿 PRICKLY THISTLE FACTS 🌿

Touchy title

Scottish monarchs were always called King or Queen of Scots (rather than King or Queen of Scotland) because of the Declaration of Arbroath in 1320, when Robert the Bruce was declared king. At that time the Scottish nobles said that if the king didn't look after his people, they would get rid of him and find someone better. It meant the king was ruler of the people, not owner of the land.

Scotland ♥ France

James V needed some powerful allies against his English uncle Henry. He decided to strengthen his ties with France by marrying a French princess. Scotland had a long tradition of being friends with France – they called it the 'auld alliance' – because France had a long tradition of being enemies with England. France often supported the Scots against the English.

James's first wife, Madeleine, was a daughter of the French king. She was frail and beautiful and she died a few weeks after she arrived in Scotland. For his second wife he chose another Frenchwoman. Marie of Guise was a big, tough woman. At one stage, before James came on the scene, Uncle Henry had fancied her for a wife himself.

Marie was a widow and when she came to Scotland she left behind her son, Francis, to be cared for by her family in France. Marie and James had two sons, but one died as a baby and the other as a toddler. Then, while Marie was pregnant with her third child, war broke out between England and Scotland again. This time the excuse was that Henry wanted James to support him in his struggle against the Pope. The Scots were defeated at the battle of Solway Moss in 1542, and James went into a decline.

James was right. The news of Mary's birth, a week before his death, hadn't cheered him up at all. The Scottish crown had once come into the Stewart family via a woman (after lowly Walter Stewart married into the royal family – in the shape of Robert the Bruce's daughter – in the fourteenth century), and James thought the family would lose it via a woman too.

11

James didn't have as many wives as his uncle, Henry VIII, but he had more children. And while Uncle Hal kept changing his mind about who he'd legally been married to, James most definitely wasn't married to the mothers of most of his children. (He had had six children before his first marriage in 1540.)

Mary had six older half-brothers, but she was James's only legitimate living child, so she inherited the throne.

Scotland had another infant for its monarch, and immediately the nobles formed a Council of Regency to look after the country till baby Mary grew up.

An early engagement

Mary of Guise, now Queen Mother of Scotland, wrote to her mother, Antoinette, Duchess of Guise…

Dearest Mama,

A brief note at this sad time. Do not believe the rumours you hear. Mary is a beautiful, healthy baby.

Yes, it does look as if the Protestants among the barons (one can hardly call the leaders of the Scottish families 'nobles' – they are far too rough and common) are getting the upper hand, but that may work in our favour. I hear that King Henry of England wants baby Mary to marry his son Edward. Sir Ralph Sadler, the English ambassador, came to visit the other day and I had Mary brought to see him. She lay smiling and gurgling at him, as I bade the nurse undress her fully so that Sir Ralph could see there was nothing wrong with her. He thought she was a gorgeous baby so let's hope it works out. We could do a lot worse, and the Scottish Protestants may even agree to it!

Give darling Francis my love and tell him to write to his mama.

I remain your dutiful and affectionate daughter,
Marie

Marie of Guise was right. Henry was dead keen to marry baby Mary to Prince Edward (aged six). It would mean that when Henry was dead and gone, Edward and Mary could rule England and Scotland as joint King and Queen. And more importantly, Henry could in the meantime rule both countries on behalf of both of them.

The Scottish Protestants weren't keen on that bit. But within a year, the situation in Scotland had changed and the Catholics had the upper hand. They didn't want an alliance with England, so they refused to sign the treaty that Henry had drawn up. Mary's first engagement was off – and she wasn't even a year old.

THE SCOTTISH HERALD

10 September 1543

BAIRN CROWNED QUEEN OF SCOTS

Three earls descended from James I held the royal insignia o' Scotland at the coronation of a nine-month-old bairn in the chapel of Stirling Castle yesterday. Mathew Stewart, Earl of Lennox, carried the sceptre, Jamie Hamilton, Earl of Arran, bore the crown; while the Earl of Argyll carried the sword.

The crown was over-big for the bairn's head, so after the anointing with oil, Hamilton held it high above the wean as the nobles called out, 'God bless the Queen!'

Some folk were asking who had chosen the date for the coronation. 'Do they no remember this is the anniversary of the Battle o' Flodden Field?' asked Angus MacBain, a local candlemaker, aged 27. 'It disnae seem to me a great date to choose. Could they no have waited till the morn?'

In the words of the English ambassador:

> The baby was crowned with such solemnitie as they do use in this country, which is not very costlie.

Darling Mama,

Your pretty little granddaughter was crowned yesterday. A dismal little ceremony, though of course one wouldn't dare say that out loud.

As you know, all hope has faded for a match with the English princeling. As I saw our darling surrounded by these fierce men, all swearing to protect her, I felt a terrible fear. To me they looked like wolves, and I fear the fangs of their ambition will tear our darling to death.

How I wish we were home in France. I think so often of the fun of my youth and wonder why it is I have to live out my days here in this cold and misty land, among 'nobles' who are for the most part no better than bandits.

Love to my beloved Francis if you see him, and beg him to write to his Mama.

I remain your dutiful and affectionate daughter,
Marie

Henry VIII was furious with the Scots for breaking off Mary's engagement to his son. He decided it was time to put the boot in again. English troops poured over the border, destroying the border towns, then attacking and burning Edinburgh, and sacking the royal palace of Holyrood. Baby Mary had to be moved from castle to castle to avoid being taken prisoner by the English.

WE'RE GOING TO RUN OUT OF CASTLES SOON...

Religious division

To Marie of Guise, the obvious solution was that Mary should be promised in marriage to a French prince. Then the French would be duty-bound to help the Scots against the English. This didn't suit the Protestant lords, because France was a mainly Catholic country.

It's hard now to realize how vile people once were to each other simply for believing in the 'wrong' sort of religion, but at that time Christians were at each other's throats all over Europe. In Scotland the Catholics were led by Cardinal Beaton, and the Protestants by George Wishart and John Knox.

THE SCOTTISH HERALD

March 1546

WISHART DEAD BY FIRE

Cardinal Beaton and his bishops bade their lackeys bring cushioned seats out on to the walls of St Andrews castle today. Then their lordships sat and watched gentle George Wishart, the Protestant preacher, go up in flames.

Feeling was running high in the town as Wishart burned at the stake for his beliefs.

'Thon fancy cardinal had better watch his back,' said one onlooker who wouldn't give his name.

THE SCOTTISH HERALD

June 1546

BEATON'S BODY HUNG FROM TOWER

Gentle George Wishart was avenged today – by a group of lairds who had sworn to kill Cardinal Beaton.

The Cardinal was having some building work done at St Andrews Castle. His gatekeeper did not suspect a thing when a gang of masons arrived at their work. He let them into the castle – and too late discovered that they weren't builders at all! The men found the Cardinal (who had taken a vow of chastity when he joined the priesthood) in bed with a girlfriend. They dragged him from the room, and held a sword at his throat as they told him why they must kill him. Then they fell on him with swords and hacked him to death.

Now his battered body hangs from a tower at St Andrews Castle – a savage warning no tae kill any more Protestant preachers.

The lairds are in charge of the castle and they mean to stay that way.

'I dinnae hold wi' violence,' said Mistress Tait, who lives near the castle, 'but if anyin had it coming to him, that yin did.'

This story shows some of the reasons why so many people were opposed to the Catholic church in the sixteenth century. A lot of priests were not living like men of God – they weren't keeping their vows, and they were rich and powerful. At the same time, the Catholic church was harsh and cruel towards people who didn't believe exactly as it did. They justified their cruelty by saying they were saving people from hellfire and eternal damnation.

Catholic troops now came after Beaton's murderers. They besieged St Andrews Castle, but the Protestant lairds held on in there, hoping for English reinforcements. In the end it was the Catholic French, invited by Marie of Guise, who recaptured St Andrews and packed the Protestant lairds off to France as prisoners.

New kings

Henry VIII died in January 1547. The new King of England, Edward VI, was only 10 so he wasn't making too many decisions. Instead his uncle, the Duke of Somerset, came rampaging up to Scotland with an English army for another battle fixture with the Scots. Life was so dangerous that little Queen Mary had to be removed from Stirling Castle and taken to a priory on the island of Inchmahome till the English had gone back to England for the winter.

The King of France also died in 1547. The new King, Henry II, wanted to keep in with the powerful Guise family. What better way than by marrying his three-year-old son to four-year-old Mary Stewart, granddaughter of the Duke of Guise? With the Scots beginning to realize they couldn't defeat the English on their own, a deal was made. Mary would marry Henry II's son and heir, the Dauphin, Francis; she would go to live and be brought up in France; and French troops would come to Scotland to help defend Scotland against the English.

OVER THE SEA TO FRANCE

Poor old Marie of Guise! When she came to Scotland to marry James V, she had been heart-broken to leave her young son behind. Now in July 1548, little Princess Mary, who was just over five and half, set sail in a French ship. Marie couldn't go with her. She had to stay and rule Scotland with the Scottish nobles (or try to…)

Little Mary didn't travel on her own. She had a lot of servants – two guardians, a nursemaid, a governess, a chaplain (who stayed with her all her life without pay), plus an armed escort of Scottish lords.

There was also a whole procession of child-courtiers.

There were four more Marys – Mary Beaton, Mary Seton, Mary Livingston and Mary Fleming, whose mum was governess to our Mary. Then there were her two older half-brothers, James and Robert, plus a whole lot of other little boys. (One of them, Mary Seton's brother, died soon after they reached France.) So all in all, it was a bit like an infant school trip which was going to last a lo-o-ong time.

It was a dramatic trip.

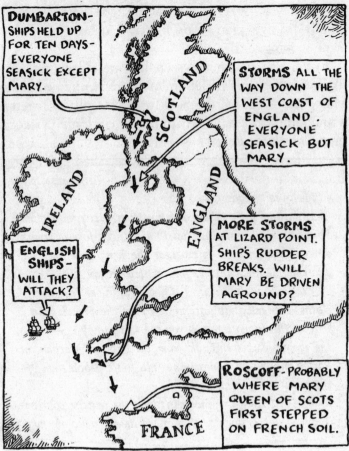

DUMBARTON – SHIPS HELD UP FOR TEN DAYS – EVERYONE SEASICK EXCEPT MARY.

STORMS ALL THE WAY DOWN THE WEST COAST OF ENGLAND. EVERYONE SEASICK BUT MARY.

ENGLISH SHIPS – WILL THEY ATTACK?

MORE STORMS AT LIZARD POINT. SHIP'S RUDDER BREAKS. WILL MARY BE DRIVEN AGROUND?

ROSCOFF – PROBABLY WHERE MARY QUEEN OF SCOTS FIRST STEPPED ON FRENCH SOIL.

SCOTLAND

IRELAND

ENGLAND

FRANCE

When they reached France there were more accidents. At one town, the drawbridge collapsed and a lot of Mary's horsemen ended up in the moat. Soon after

everyone got ill. Then the French commander who was escorting Mary was called away to fight with Henry II. Finally, Mary's gran, Antoinette, Duchess of Guise, came looking for her.

Antoinette had never seen her granddaughter but, like everyone else, she fell in love with her immediately. Mary was a real picture-book princess, tall and pretty, with long fair hair. Antoinette couldn't wait to introduce her at court.

August 1548

My beloved daughter,

Your darling girl is safely arrived. What a charming child! Such beautiful skin! Such hair! Such a well-formed mouth! And so intelligent! I know that the King of France will adore her. A great fiancée for his little froggy son!

She will, of course, need a new wardrobe. The Scottish clothes are really not quite up to life at the French court. I will set this in motion, and you can settle up with me when the money comes through from the Scottish Parliament. Such a bore, when monarchs have to go the people to beg for the clothes they stand up in.

And I do see what you mean about the Scottish courtiers. They are all très sauvage. Not one of them is what one might call courtly. And your little darling has no language but Scots. May I take the liberty, therefore, of dismissing Lady Fleming, who seems a bit temperamental, from her post and substituting a more elegant French governess in her place?

My darling girl, I look forward to hearing from you.

Your loving Mama

September 1548

Dearest Mama,

So glad to hear that Mary arrived safely, and that everyone loves her as much as I do myself. I am so happy that you are able to look after her, and that she seems content to be in her mama's country. And yes, you must do as you see fit with regard to her wardrobe. I have been out in the wilds so long I no longer know what is fashionable at court.

However, I beg you, do not dismiss Lady Fleming. She is not at all like the other Scots, and I am anxious that Mary keep her Scots tongue. From all accounts, the little French boy is not in good health. God forbid anything should happen to him, but if it does, then one day she may return and rule this dank and misty kingdom.

I hope that by the time you receive this letter Mary will have been presented to the little Dauphin, and perhaps even have met her father-in-law to be. Pray write and give me news of the event.

Your loving daughter,

Marie

The French court

December 1548

Dearest Mama,
Yesterday I met my fiancé. His name is Francis he is a year younger than me he is a bit fat and has a cough but I like him anyway.
I miss you darling Mama
Your loving daughter
Mary
xxxxx

COUGH COUGH

December 1548

Dearest Marie,
Everything is going wonderfully well! As you know, your brother Francis was married yesterday, and the royal family were all invited to the wedding. The little Dauphin attended, with his sisters and his Mama. He met our darling Mary for the first time, and they danced a gavotte together.

Little Monsieur was clearly very taken with her and she seemed not in the least put out by his runny nose and his rather pale, swollen appearance. Even the ghastly Catherine de Medici, who thinks nothing and no one is worthy of her own brood, seemed charmed by our little darling.

The King has decreed that Mary is to share a room with his own darling daughter, Princess Elisabeth, for he wants them to be best of friends! And in royal processions she is to precede his own children, quite rightly, as she is an anointed queen.

Everything is going very well. I know you miss your little darling, but just think what her marriage will do for the family.

I remain, your ever-loving Mama

Mary was more-or-less adopted by the French royal family. She lived with the royal children and was thoroughly spoilt. Meanwhile, the four other Marys were all packed off to a French convent to be educated.

WAS IT SOMETHING WE SAID?

KING HENRY II OF FRANCE. MAD KEEN ON HUNTING, NOT TO MENTION WINE AND WOMEN. HE WAS FROM THE HOUSE OF VALOIS, WHO WERE THE BIG RIVALS OF THE GUISES AND THE BOURBONS.

FRANCIS, ELDEST SON. A SEMI-INVALID, SMALL AND BLOATED. EVEN HIS DOTING MUM SAID HE NEEDED TO BLOW HIS NOSE MORE OFTEN. THIS WAS THE FROG THAT MARY WOULD MARRY— BUT NOT EVEN A KISS FROM HER WOULD TURN HIM INTO A HANDSOME PRINCE.

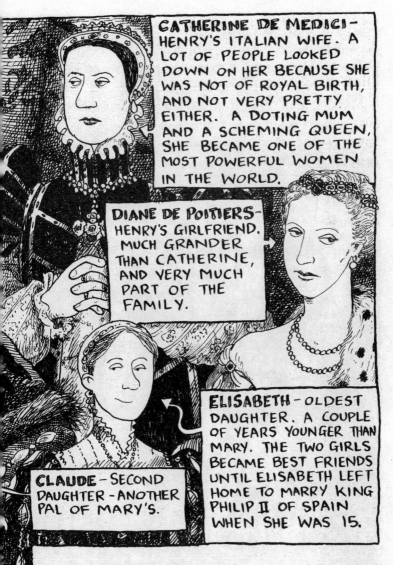

CATHERINE DE MEDICI - HENRY'S ITALIAN WIFE. A LOT OF PEOPLE LOOKED DOWN ON HER BECAUSE SHE WAS NOT OF ROYAL BIRTH, AND NOT VERY PRETTY EITHER. A DOTING MUM AND A SCHEMING QUEEN, SHE BECAME ONE OF THE MOST POWERFUL WOMEN IN THE WORLD.

DIANE DE POITIERS - HENRY'S GIRLFRIEND. MUCH GRANDER THAN CATHERINE, AND VERY MUCH PART OF THE FAMILY.

ELISABETH - OLDEST DAUGHTER. A COUPLE OF YEARS YOUNGER THAN MARY. THE TWO GIRLS BECAME BEST FRIENDS UNTIL ELISABETH LEFT HOME TO MARRY KING PHILIP II OF SPAIN WHEN SHE WAS 15.

CLAUDE - SECOND DAUGHTER - ANOTHER PAL OF MARY'S.

Henry and Catherine went on to have four more children after Mary joined the family including Charles and Henry (both of whom later became kings of France).

27

Mary's Guise relations

As well as the royal family, which Mary only belonged to because she was engaged to the Dauphin, her own mum's family played a big part in her upbringing.

Mary's mum came from one of the most clannish, ambitious and powerful families in France – the Guise family (pronounced Geez) – who saw in little Mary their passport to POWER!

Gran, a.k.a. Antoinette, Duchess of Guise

She married at 15 and over the next 20 years produced 12 children. Now pushing 50, and a widow, she dressed all in black, and kept her coffin in the corridor so it would be handy when she needed it. (As it turned out, she didn't need it for quite a while – she lived to be 89!)

Uncle Francis, Duke of Guise

Antoinette's eldest son. Clever, ambitious, always one eye on the main chance. Francis was married to Anne d'Este, who got on well with Mary.

Uncle Charles, Cardinal of Lorraine

Said to be cunning and greedy. He gave Mary lessons in statecraft – which means he taught her how to play one enemy off against another, and think three steps ahead of everyone else. Judging by the way her life turned out, he didn't make a very good job of it.

There were also assorted other uncles and aunts. They all stuck to Mary like glue while she was Dauphiness-to-be, but later on, when Francis had snuffed it, they weren't so keen on following her to Scotland.

The royal nursery

The children of the House of Valois had a right royal upbringing. At that time, Italian architects and painters were coming to France to build and decorate fabulous palaces and gardens. It was warm, it was sunny, their royal parents adored them, and they and all their pets and all their servants and all their clothes moved from posh palace to posh palace. One thing that wasn't more sophisticated than in England or Scotland however, was the toilet. That was the main reason for moving on. The bogs got bunged up. So the royal noses wouldn't be offended by the pong, the royal cavalcade went elsewhere, leaving lesser mortals to sort out the loos.

Dearest Mama

I want to tell you about my most favourite palace of all. It is called Anet, and it belongs to Tante Diane. We have all been staying there, even the babies.

Guess how many dogs we have with us! 28! Four big ones, and the rest little ones. And the other day someone kindly gave us two bears, though I do not think we can keep them with us, for they keep damaging the furniture and pooing everywhere.

Elizabeth, Claude and I are rehearsing a masquerade with which we will entertain the whole court. I like acting and singing very much, and everyone says that I have a beautiful voice. I am also a really good dancer.

You asked about Francis' health—

well, he is better now it is summer, but
he gets many colds and often has
earache. Did I tell you that he has five
doctors now? Unfortunately they all
give him different medicines so he has
to take a lot. He is a poor sickly prince,
but don't worry, I love him just the same.
And he loves me, and often talks about
when we shall be married.

Lady Fleming tells me she will have to
go back to Scotland as she is not well, so
I am to have a new governess, Madame
de Parois. I am studying as well as
I can, but I do not especially like my
lessons. It is so much more fun to
dance and sing and hunt.

your daughter Mary xx

In fact, Lady Fleming was being sent home in disgrace
because she was pregnant with King Henry's baby. Both
Catherine de Medici and Diane de Poitiers took a dim
view of that, so she had to go. And Mary didn't get on
with the new governess. As she became a teenager Mary
started to throw a few wobblies. She was energetic and
sporty most of the time but some weeks she overdid it
and then she got ill and had go to bed for a few days.
This went on all through her life.

Mary gets hitched

1558 was a big year for Mary. She was 15, which in those days was considered old enough for girls to marry. The Dauphin was only 14, and a pretty puny 14 at that. But they were both royal so their marriage was more about foreign affairs than love. King Henry II wanted the marriage so that he could call on Scottish troops to help him fight England. And all those Guise uncles wanted it so that the marriage was safely in the bag after all the years of waiting.

It was something of a bonus that Mary and Francis actually liked each other!

KING HENRY AND QUEEN CATHERINE ARE HAPPY TO ANNOUNCE THE FORTHCOMING MARRIAGE OF THEIR ELDEST SON, THE DAUPHIN FRANCIS TO MARY, QUEEN OF SCOTS. THE MARRIAGE WILL TAKE PLACE NEXT SUNDAY, 24 APRIL IN NOTRE DAME CATHEDRAL PARIS.

ALLÔ!

Avril 1558

It has been called the most romantic marriage of the century. Childhood sweethearts Mary (hounded from her own country by the perfidious English) and Francis (heir to the French throne) were joined in Holy Matrimony by the Archbishop of Rouen, in the presence of the Bishop of Paris.

Onlookers packed the stands (specially built by the Bishop for the occasion) around the cathedral. They waited for hours for a glimpse of the beautiful bride – and were rewarded by one of the most magnificent pageants of all time. First came the Swiss Guards, followed by

33

musicians, liveried in yellow and red, playing violins, trumpets, fifes and drums. Then came the king's private retinue of 100 gentlemen-in-waiting. Next the royal princes, cousins of the bridegroom, all gorgeously arrayed in silk and velvet. Princes were followed by prelates, and then came the bridegroom himself, the Dauphin Francis, flanked by his younger brothers, the Dukes of Orleans and Angoulême.

Gasps went up from spectators and guests alike as the bride herself arrived. The Queen of Scotland wore a dress of white, which showed off to perfection her creamy skin and magnificent auburn hair. Her long train was borne by two ladies-in-waiting as tall and willowy as the Queen herself. At her neck were diamonds; on her head a crown of gold, decorated with pearls, rubies and sapphires. The Queen smiled and waved graciously to her well-wishers as she entered the church.

Next came all the ladies of the court, dressed in gorgeous silks and satins. As they disappeared inside the cathedral, people in the stands crowded around the windows for a glimpse of the ceremony.

Afterwards, there was the traditional distribution of 'largesse' as the King's heralds threw gold coins into the crowds. Then it was back to the palace, where the curtains were left open so that the ordinary folk could glimpse guests at the magnificent banquet. Halfway through the spectacular ball that followed, six golden galleons with silver sails slid into the ballroom. A masked prince in each galleon invited each of the royal ladies aboard and they sailed around the ballroom to the delight of the hundreds of guests.

Mary arrives in her white dress, embroidered with diamonds and sapphires, under a blue velvet cloak edged with ermine.

The royal couple celebrated in style at the palace.

Lord Brantôme, an eyewitness at the wedding, was bowled over by Mary…

> *She appeared a hundred times more beautiful than a goddess of heaven… If the kingdom of Scotland was anything of a prize, the Queen was far more precious thanit, for even if she had neither sceptre nor crown, her person alone was worth a kingdom.*

He wasn't the only one. Lots of French people thought the young Scottish Queen was incredibly romantic. They called her La Reine Blanche (the White Queen) because she wore white whenever possible. It caused quite a stir when she wore it at her wedding, because in France it was the colour of mourning.

Of course, not everyone was thrilled by the royal wedding. France was hard up, because she had been in endless wars, so a lot of people thought the wedding was a waste of money. They stuck anonymous letters and poems up on doors saying what they felt.

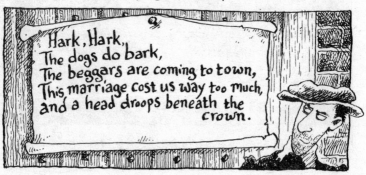

Hark, Hark,
The dogs do bark,
The beggars are coming to town,
This marriage cost us way too much,
and a head droops beneath the
                              crown.

Mary's head really did droop beneath the heavy crown and as the day wore on, the crown had to be removed and held for her by a lord-in-waiting.

But the people who complained about the wedding were wrong that the government had footed the whole bill. A lot of it was paid for by Mary's uncle, the Duke of Guise.

The secret treaty

Before royals could marry, there always had to be marriage treaties. The Scots would have been none too pleased about the marriage treaty Mary's mum had drawn up with France – if they had known what it was. For when Mary married Francis, there were two marriage treaties.

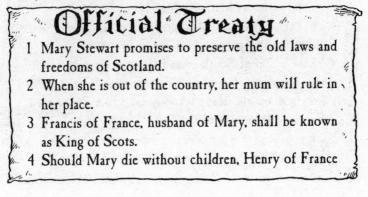

Official Treaty

1 Mary Stewart promises to preserve the old laws and freedoms of Scotland.

2 When she is out of the country, her mum will rule in her place.

3 Francis of France, husband of Mary, shall be known as King of Scots.

4 Should Mary die without children, Henry of France

and his son Francis promise faithfully to promote the succession of the Scot nearest in blood to the Queen.

5 When Francis becomes King of France the kingdoms of France and Scotland shall be united, and subjects of either monarch may live in both countries.

6 Should Francis die, Mary will receive a pension of 600,000 crowns; she may choose whether to live in France or return to Scotland.

7 The eldest male heir of Francis and Mary, will inherit the thrones of Scotland and France. In the absence of a male heir, any female child will inherit the throne of Scotland only.

8 The crown of Scotland will be sent to France for safekeeping.

As you can see, everyone was pretty interested in collecting crowns but France was interested in much more than the crown…

SECRET TREATY

1 If Mary dies without children…

a) her claim to the throne of England will automatically pass to the King of France

b) the realm of Scotland and all its taxes will pass to the King of France, until such time as the debt incurred by the King of France in the defence of Scotland shall be repaid.

2 This agreement supersedes any other agreement reached between Mary Stewart and the Estates of Scotland.

Mary and Francis shared one kingdom and were lined up to share another. And, by the end of the year, Mary was laying claim to a third crown. In November her first cousin Queen Mary I of England died. Mary's heir was her half-sister, Elizabeth. But in Catholic eyes Liz was illegitimate, because her dad, Henry VIII, had been on very dodgy ground when he divorced Mary's mum to marry Liz's. And if Liz – who was Protestant – was illegitimate, guess who was heir to the throne of England? None other than our heroine, Mary Queen of Scots.

King Henry II decided to stake her claim for her. He declared his daughter-in-law Queen of England and Ireland as well as Scotland. To ram the point home, he had a new coat-of-arms made for Mary, with the arms of England, Ireland, Scotland and France quartered on it.

It did absolutely nothing for Mary's relationship with her cousin Liz.

And the day was coming, all too soon, when Mary would need Elizabeth for a friend.

PRICKLY THISTLE FACT

Stewarts and Stuarts

The name Stewart comes from the word 'steward'. The first Stewarts were originally stewards to the Scottish royal family. Stewards weren't just people who served the drinks. They were more like estate managers, and over time they became more and more important and had lands of their own. One of them, Walter Stewart, married the daughter of Robert the Bruce, and their son became the first Stewart King of Scots.

Mary changed the spelling of her name from Stewart to Stuart when she lived in France. This was because the French don't have the letter 'w' and couldn't get the pronunciation right.

She kept the spelling 'Stuart' when she came back to Scotland – and all her descendants kept it too. Her son James was the first of the Stuart Kings of England.

QUEEN OF FRANCE

THE SCOTS QUEEN IS A COMELY LASS
HER HAIR COMES TUMBLING DOWN.
SHE RIDES AND HUNTS AND DANCES-OH
THE TOAST OF EVERY TOWN.

THE DAUPHIN IS A FAT YOUNG BOY,
WITH SUPPURATING SKIN.
WHAT DOES THE QUEEN SEE IN
                    HIM THEN?
WHY THE CROWN SHE WEDS TO WIN!

Mary was Dauphiness for just a year. In that time, France was in a terrible state because there was no money, and civil war had broken out between Catholics and Protestants, but she and Francis carried on as if they hadn't noticed.

They did notice other things, however. Five Scottish noblemen, including Mary's oldest half-brother, James Stewart, fell ill with food poisoning on their way back to Scotland with state papers. The cure for food poisoning in those days was to hang the patient upside down.

I STILL FEEL A BIT QUEASY...

Only James Stewart survived the illness – and the treatment. Later in her life, Mary probably wished he hadn't.

And another argument had broken out about the Scottish crown. The French wanted it sent to France, so that the Dauphin could be crowned king but the Scots weren't keen to let it out of their sight.

WE CANNAE LET YOU HAVE THE REAL CROWN, BUT HERE'S AN ARTIST'S IMPRESSION...

Meanwhile, there were plans afoot for the Princess Elisabeth – Mary's best friend and now her sister-in-law – to marry King Philip of Spain. It was in the middle of preparations for this that tragedy struck.

30 June 1559

KING TAKES LANCE IN EYE

King Henry II was badly injured in the jousting lists yesterday. After a successful day at the tournament, held to celebrate the forthcoming double-wedding of his daughters Elisabeth and Claude, the king challenged the Count of Montgomery to one final joust. Crowds watched excitedly as the two men galloped towards each other at full tilt. Excitement turned to horror as the Count's lance splintered and a large piece went into the king's eye. Last night his condition was said to be serious.

3 July 1559
FOREWARNED OF TRAGEDY

It was revealed that the Queen begged King Henry not to joust in the tournament last week – her astrologer had warned her of a possible tragedy.

8 July 1559
KING DYING

Sources close to the King say that there is no hope that he will recover. A week after the accident, which left him blind in one eye, infection has set in and he is said to be delirious. However, he has given orders that the wedding of the two princesses should go ahead as planned.

The wedding took place. It was a sorry affair, with Henry at death's door. Soon pudgy Francis was King of France – and Mary was Queen. It looked as if she would produce a brood of children, and stay in France for the rest of her life. Her own kingdom, Scotland, seemed very far away.

King Francis II

19 September 1559

Dearest Mama,

Yesterday Francis was crowned. I didn't have to be, because of having been crowned when I was a baby.

It was a horrible day, wet and windy, and the ceremony was very low key because everyone was so shocked at poor father-in-law's death. Francis wore black. He looked very young and a bit scared. However, I think his Mama is going to help him govern until he is a bit older, together with my uncles Guise.

I wore a white dress for the coronation and today too I am in white, and so is everyone else. It is a sad time.

your loving daughter Mary

Mary was 16 when she became Queen of France, and a lot more clued up than her 15-year-old husband.

24 September 1559

Dear Tante Diane,

This is to say how sorry I am about poor Uncle Henry. You must be feeling very sad to lose him so suddenly.

By the way, I understand that he lent you some of the crown jewels to look after. Would you mind awfully giving them back? Technically they belong to the Queen of France, and that is now me.

Sorry to bother you at this time.

Your loving friend, Mary

Mary was also interested in government, although Francis's mum, Catherine of Medici, ran the show, with Mary's Guise uncles to help her. This didn't go down well with the man who by rights should have been Prince Regent, the Duke of Bourbon. He took up with the French Protestants, who were called Huguenots. Catherine and the Guises were fierce in putting down the rebellion. They tortured their prisoners – Catherine liked to watch – and then the prisoners were hanged right outside the palace windows after supper. Mary hated cruelty, so she didn't go near the torture chamber, but she went everywhere else with Catherine. They received ambassadors together, they went to church together, and seemed as thick as thieves, though a lot of people thought they couldn't stand the sight of one another.

In June 1560, news arrived that Mary's mother, whom she hadn't seen for nine years, had died in Scotland. Mary was distraught. She and her mum had been great pen pals, writing to each other nearly every single day, and her mum had been the one to make sure she wasn't forgotten in Scotland. With the news of her death came other bad news too – the English were attacking the port of Leith. Mary had to act for herself now. She sent messengers to conclude a treaty with the English.

The Treaty of Edinburgh

1 All English troops to back off in return for all French troops withdrawing from Scotland.

2 The King and Queen of France and Scotland to stop calling themselves King and Queen of England.

Her cousin Liz would have been really pleased about this ... if only Mary had got round to signing it! However, Mary didn't sign it, partly because husband Francis wasn't keen on giving up his title to the English throne. Claiming the English crown seems to have been one of the few aspects of government that interested him. Most of his time he spent hunting.

47

Despite all the soup and sympathy, it was no good. Francis died in December 1560 and Mary was a widow at the age of 18.

The teenage widow

Even though her husband was nobody's idea of a cool dude, Mary was still really upset and as everyone else rushed about trying to get the best deal for themselves, she lay crying in her room. Then she got a letter from her mother-in-law…

6 *December, 1560*

Dearest Mary,

Just to remind you, in case you forget in the middle of all your grief, that the crown jewels are the property not of the Dowager Queen but of the King of France, i.e. my younger son Charles. Please be so good as to return them ASAP.

Your loving mother-in-law,
Catherine

The letter from Catherine told her where she stood now that Francis was dead – absolutely nowhere. The best solution to that was another husband.

Top of the list was Don Carlos, son of the King of Spain.

Carlos was even less attractive than Francis because he was greedy and cruel as well as deformed. This didn't put Mary off, but Catherine wasn't keen. She didn't want Mary allied with Spain. She wrote secret letters to her daughter

Elisabeth. In them she gave Mary a codename: 'le gentilhomme' (the gentleman).

January 1561

Darling Lisbeth,

I write to warn you that le gentilhomme is very keen on the idea of Carlos. No need to tell you that if she marries him, she could well end up in your way. God forbid that anything should happen to darling Philip, but if it did, Carlos would be king, and if le gentilhomme were married to him, guess who would be queen. Suggest you put in a bad word for her with Philip.

All my love to you, darling,
Mama

MARY'S SECRET DIARY

February 1561

What now?

1/ Stay in France?

Pro: Good climate, Catholic country (at least at the moment), Sophisticated court, better choice of husband — Carlos?

Con: Do I want to be the second Queen Dowager? Catherine hates me. Elisabeth has gone to Spain. And Claude has turned into a snobby phoney since she got married.

> 2/ Return to Scotland?
> Con: Cold, wild and wet Protestant country and they don't really want me.
> Pro: It is my own country, and I am queen there in my own right. I will soon pick up a husband especially as I am next in line to the English throne.

The Scottish Parliament – the Estates – weren't that keen on their young queen coming back. OK, so her dad had been King of Scots, but her mum was French and she had been brought up in France. As far as they were concerned, she was a French princess. In the end they said she could come, provided she didn't make them all turn Catholic. Mary wasn't about to do that. She didn't mind what religion people were, provided that she herself could continue to practise her Catholic religion in private.

50

MARY'S SECRET DIARY

July 1561

My cousin Elizabeth, has refused my safe-conduct through England. Sir William says it is because I won't sign the Treaty of Edinburgh. I told him I will sign it, one day, but not yet. For my uncle the Cardinal has told me that when you agree terms with someone you must always extract a favour in return. And if I am to give up my (very good) claim to the English throne then I must get from her an assurance that should anything

51

happen to her (God forbid!) then I will be the next Queen of England.

Liz

BURP

Mary could be a bit of a drama-queen. She enjoyed the next bit.

Monsieur l'Ambassadeur, if my preparations were not so advanced, peradventure your mistress the Queen's unkindness might stay my voyage, but now I am prepared to adventure the matter whatever come of it. I trust the wind will be so favourable as I do not need to come to the coast of England; and if I do, Monsieur l'Ambassadeur, your mistress the Queen shall have me in her hands to do her will of me; and if she be so hard-hearted as to desire my end she may then do her pleasure, and make a sacrifice of me; peradventure that casualty for me might be better for me than to live.

In other words, 'Up yours, Lizzy!' Mary decided that she would go back to Scotland the way she had come – by sea, without going anywhere near England. She said goodbye to all her pals at the French court…

…and went on board ship. A couple of her Guise uncles, and lots of French courtiers, went with her to make sure she was all right. But not all of them…

53

At the time everyone thought that Elizabeth planned to capture Mary. That was why Mary travelled by galley. Galleys were smaller and faster than sailing ships, and they didn't have to wait for the wind, because as well as sails they also had lots of oars. It meant that the bigger English ships, patrolling the seas between France and England were less likely to catch them.

In fact, the English navy came close, but didn't try to stop Mary. What Mary didn't know then was that Elizabeth never got into fights if she didn't have to, and believed passionately in the right of kings and queens to rule their own country. She just objected when they wanted to take over hers.

Nevertheless, all Mary's horses were confiscated when the ship carrying them had to put in at Tynemouth (in England).

And when Mary's ships passed Flamborough Head in Northumberland, there were so many English ships surrounding her that people on shore thought she had a whole fleet.

It was all a bit worrying, but there were no storms, and one foggy morning in August Mary arrived safely in Scotland – without her horses, but with her jewels. After 13 years in France, the Queen of Scots had come home.

THE WILD WEST OF EUROPE

Mary was only 18 years old when she landed in Scotland. It was a rude shock to her system. She was used to the French court. There the nobles were showy and sophisticated, the palaces grand and comfortable, and music, dancing, poetry and beautiful clothes were right at the top of the agenda.

The Scots were a very different story. Their castles were mostly dark and cold, and many of the Scottish nobles never got out of their hunting gear. As for wooing and romantic love ... well, just wait and see what happens to Mary.

From the start, Mary had three big problems when it came to dealing with her new country.

1 She was a woman. Women had a tough time as rulers anywhere, but Scotland was the rugged Wild West of Europe, and the men bossed the women around even more than usual.

2 She was Catholic. Under Marie of Guise many of the Scots nobles had turned Protestant. Power was in the hands of a little group who called themselves Lords of

the Congregation, and they weren't too thrilled to have their queen back.

3 She was an outsider. She had been brought up in France. This meant she didn't have a hope of understanding all the family squabbles that passed for politics in sixteenth-century Scotland.

But her first problem was that there was no one to meet her…

THE SCOTTISH HERALD
19 August 1561
SURPRISE ARRIVAL

Leith merchant, Andrew Lambie, had a surprise guest this morning, when Queen Mary of Scots arrived in her capital city a week earlier than expected.

It was a damp, foggy morning, and the streets were empty when two small, fast galleys rowed up the Firth of Forth and tied up in Leith Harbour.

Dockers and fishermen watched in amazement, as a large, glamorous group of men and women – chattering away in French – disembarked from the galleys on to the cobbled dockside. Richly dressed in bright satins and velvets, they made the Leith docks on a damp morning look drabber than ever. Standing out among them because of her height and beauty was the young and beautiful 18-year-old Queen.

'Ye'd hae thocht they could hae sent someone doon here to welcome her,' said Willie Dalgliesh, a sailor, who watched the Queen's arrival from a nearby ship. But a spokesman for Lord James Stewart, the Queen's older half-brother, said that the Queen had arrived much sooner than expected. 'They had following winds, and made excellent time,' he said. 'No one thought they would be here for another four or five days. But we're delighted to see her anyway.'

Not only was there no gun salute to welcome the Queen, but the Palace of Holyrood was not ready either. So the Queen and exotic retinue were escorted to the house of local merchant, Andrew Lambie, 52.

Asked later what he made of the young Queen, Mr Lambie, who had known the Queen's mother, said she was 'a bonnie lassie'. He said that he and the Queen had spoken in Scots. 'She stayed at my house all day and then, towards evening, her brother came together with the Earl o' Argyll and Lord Erskine, and they put on a wee bit of a procession to take her up to Holyrood,' said Mr Lambie.

'That's a bit more like it,' said Davy Russell, a lad who works in the docks, as the streets of Leith resounded with horses' hooves.

Mary's French courtiers, however, weren't too impressed, even by the procession.

That night, as Mary went to bed in Holyrood Palace, some of her Protestant subjects came to sing psalms all night long outside the Palace on fiddles and bagpipes.

The Scottish nobles

Considering she was a Catholic queen in a Protestant country, Mary got off to quite a good start. The common people took to her in a big way. She spoke to them in their own language, and they thought she was fantastic – young, charming, pretty. However, Scotland had been chaotic for the past 20 years, and it wasn't about to change in a hurry. The nobles were more interested in their alliances and squabbles with each other than they were in forming a united front behind their queen.

There were a lot of nobles, so we'll meet them a few at a time...

1 Lord James Stewart (later Earl of Moray)

Mary's eldest half-brother, the one who had been hung upside down to get over his food poisoning. Brought up in France, he was relatively 'civilized', though with a wild streak. He defended Mary's right to worship privately as a Catholic – at least to start with. But really he thought that he should be king. If his mum had been married to his dad he would have been.

2 James Hamilton, Earl of Arran (later Duke of Chaterherault)

Heir to the throne, he'd been an ally of Mary's mum till 1554; in 1559 he joined the Protestant Lords of the Congregation, and became the leader of the Protestant party.

3 Lord William Maitland of Lethington

Shrewd, clever and ruthless, he impressed both Queen Elizabeth and her top minister William Cecil down in

England, but at home he was nicknamed Mitchell Wylie – Scots pronunciation for Machiavelli, the Italian who was famous for saying princes could do anything they liked (however nasty) if it led to stable government. Maitland did at least believe in something apart from his own power – he wanted to see a union between Scotland and England.

4 James Douglas, Earl of Morton
A nasty bit of work, calculating and cruel, who'd signed up to the Protestant faith in 1557.

5 James Hepburn, Earl of Bothwell
A Protestant, but he had supported Marie of Guise in her struggle against the other Protestants. A tough customer, ugly but attractive, he had a string of girlfriends and was supposed to dabble in witchcraft. (Later warden of Dunbar Castle, Sheriff of Edinburgh, Duke of Orkney and Shetland, *and* Mary's husband.)

PRICKLY THISTLE FACT

Why are so many of them called James?
The Scottish custom was to call the eldest son after the father's father and the eldest daughter after the mother's mother. It meant there weren't a lot of new names – particularly as some of these guys were descended from the same grandfather!

Apart from showing her own people who was boss – or trying to – Mary had two ambitions in her first year. These were:

1 To meet her cousin Elizabeth in person and persuade her to name Mary as heir to the English throne.
2 To marry herself off to some powerful ruler.

In a way the two things were intertwined, because as heir to the English throne, she was more likely to net a decent husband. The trouble was, if she seemed too Catholic, there was no way she would be named as Lizzy's successor, and if she seemed too Protestant, she would rule out most of the powerful European rulers for a husband.

It was all a bit of a balancing act for Mary, and that may explain why – unlike most kings and queens of the time – she was happy to let her subjects remain Protestants, even though she herself was a Catholic.

In actual fact, she didn't have a hope of turning Scotland back to Catholicism. The Protestant lords had got too used to running the show. Besides, she had another very bossy man to contend with. His name was John Knox, and he wasn't even a noble.

John Knox

Knox was a follower of George Wishart (the chap who was burned at the stake by Archbishop Beaton) and had been one of the men who had avenged Wishart by killing Beaton. For that he'd been sentenced to be a galley oarsman for a few years. Today we would call him a Fundamentalist – he thought he had a hotline to God. He tried to lay down the law to Mary, and she tried to lay the law down back – after all she was the queen.

Trouble blew up on her very first Sunday.

MARY'S SECRET DIARY

What an awful start! When we tried to celebrate Mass this morning – my uncles Guise and the rest of the household – a vile thug of a man, called Patrick Lindsay came rushing through the streets at the head of a noisy mob all shouting that the celebration of the Mass 'pierced the hearts of all' and screaming that they would lynch my poor priest. Thank goodness for brother James, who made up for the fact that he was not at Leith to meet me by placing himself between the mob and the chapel door — we were all inside at the time, wondering what was going to happen next. Then my half-brothers John and Robert escorted the poor terrified priest back to his rooms. I swear, had they not been there, there would have been bloodshed. But even as I write, there is a mob outside the palace gates, screaming and yelling about Papists and idolators. I shall have to act quickly to reassure them that I do not mean to force my religion on them...

Next day Mary made her first proclamation:

IT IS THE DECREE OF QUEEN MARY THAT NO ONE WILL CHANGE THE RELIGIOUS SITUATION IN SCOTLAND UNTIL THE ESTATES MEET AGAIN; IN RETURN, NO ONE IS TO THREATEN OR INTERFERE WITH HER FRENCH SERVANTS.

DANG DANG

The following Sunday, Mary tried to keep the peace by going to a Protestant service, but John Knox wasn't interested in peace-keeping.

THE SCOTTISH HERALD

Souvenir Edition   3 September 1561

WELCOME HOME, MA'AM

Yesterday saw the first official appearance of Mary, Queen of Scots, since her return from France. Crowds lined the streets to catch a glimpse of Her Majesty as she rode the Royal Mile from Holyrood House to Edinburgh Castle for a banquet attended by the nobility and distinguished citizens of Edinburgh.

Here are the highlights of the day in pictures:

Her Majesty travelling back down the Royal Mile. The magnificent velvet canopy was carried by 12 of the city magistrates.

50 young men dressed as Moors followed the Queen.

The burgesses of the city, in their royal best.

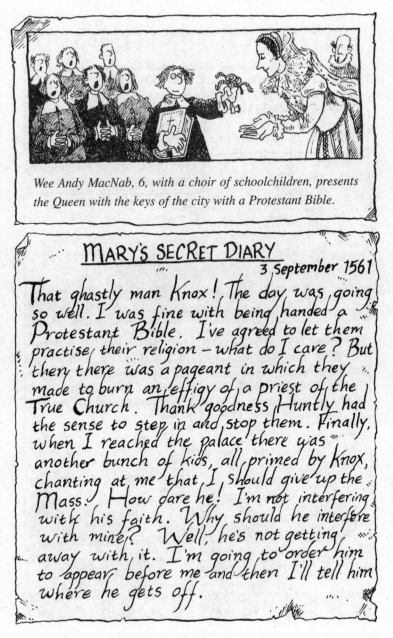

Wee Andy MacNab, 6, with a choir of schoolchildren, presents the Queen with the keys of the city with a Protestant Bible.

MARY'S SECRET DIARY
3 September 1561

That ghastly man Knox! The day was going so well. I was fine with being handed a Protestant Bible. I've agreed to let them practise their religion – what do I care? But then there was a pageant in which they made to burn an effigy of a priest of the True Church. Thank goodness Huntly had the sense to step in and stop them. Finally, when I reached the palace there was another bunch of kids, all primed by Knox, chanting at me that I should give up the Mass. How dare he! I'm not interfering with his faith. Why should he interfere with mine? Well, he's not getting away with it. I'm going to order him to appear before me and then I'll tell him where he gets off.

Mary did summon Knox to the palace and they had a real ding-dong.

69

A Highland revolt

It wasn't only the Protestants who gave Mary grief. The Catholics couldn't work out why she wasn't sticking up for the old religion. And some of them were great lairds like the Earl of Huntly, who had given Mary's mum a lot of trouble. Mary's brother wanted to show him who was boss – and Mary herself could see that he needed to be taught a lesson.

Like most Scottish sagas of this time, the trouble started in an inn. One of Huntly's sons, Lord John Gordon, who was drop-dead gorgeous and wild with it, had a fight over some land he had nicked from the Ogilvy family. He left young Ogilvy badly wounded. LJG was arrested and shut up in the Tolbooth, but not for long – he soon escaped and took to the hills. (There were a lot of hills in LJG's life. His dad owned most of the Highlands.)

MARY'S SECRET DIARY

8 August 1562

Have been ill in bed for days. After all the talk of us meeting in York, cousin Liz has called it off because of the trouble in France. It is such a pity. I know that, if I could meet her, she would come round to me and make me her heir. However, York is off, so I have decided to go hunting. Brother James says we should go north so I can see the Highlands. He says the scenery is fantastic and the hunting even better. Also he says it will

be a great opportunity to track down John Gordon and show him who's boss.
I'm glad I have James to help me and tell me what to do. I think I'll reward him by making him Earl of Moray.

That's exactly what Mary did – and Lord James Stewart went by the name of Moray from then on.

News soon got around that Mary and her party were hunting in the Highlands – and not only for deer. The Countess of Huntly, John Gordon's mum, came to see her to ask her not to be too hard on her naughty boy. Mary said, 'Fine, provided he turns himself in within a week.'

LJG wasn't about to do that – in fact, he and his men started attacking Mary's baggage train. Now it was LJG's dad's turn to suck up to Mary. He said he was disgusted at his son's behaviour and would she like some help to capture LJG? Mary said, 'Fine, bring your men and we'll hunt him down together.' That was the last she heard from him. Moray had sent for reinforcements down south, and when they arrived and took Huntly's castle, they found it stripped – apart from the chapel, which they knew Mary wouldn't touch because she, like them, was a Catholic.

Now both father and son were on the run. It would have taken Mary years to catch them if they'd stayed on the moors, but Huntly decided to attack Aberdeen. All his men deserted to Mary, and Huntly and his two sons were captured.

71

THE SCOTTISH HERALD

27 October 1562

HUNTLEY DROPS DEAD!

Queen Mary's troops, led by her brother the Earl of Moray, won a resounding victory near Aberdeen today over the powerful Gordon clan. Then – as he was brought before the Queen's generals, his hands tied behind his back – the Earl of Huntly keeled over, and fell dead from his horse.

The Earl of Huntly and his two sons had led their men into open battle with the Queen's troops, hoping that the Queen's men would defect. But as the Gordon clansmen came under fire they found themselves fleeing over marshy ground, and many of them went over to the Queen's side. The Earl's sudden death is thought to have been the result of a stroke. It spares him the traitor's death he would most certainly have faced had he lived.

The Earl of Huntly had a merciful release. LJG wasn't so lucky. He was executed.

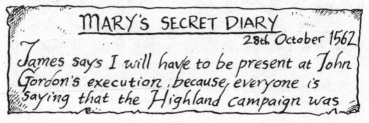

MARY'S SECRET DIARY

28th October 1562

James says I will have to be present at John Gordon's execution, because everyone is saying that the Highland campaign was

> *just a private fight between him and the Gordon family. So I have agreed. James is acting in my best interests, I know, but I'm really dreading it. I hate blood.*

The executioner made a mess of cutting off Lord John's head. Mary was completely shattered and passed out from shock. She had to be carried out, screaming and crying. LJG's younger brother, Adam, was let off – and later became one of Mary's most loyal supporters.

PRICKLY THISTLE FACT

Traitor in a pickle

Men who rebelled against the queen were traitors, and the lands of traitors were always forfeit to the crown. But the traitor was supposed to appear before the Estates so that his lands could be formally taken from him. This was a bit difficult in the case of the Earl of Huntly, who'd avoided trial and execution by dropping dead so dramatically. So his corpse was pickled in a barrel and brought before Parliament to stand trial the following year.

OOPS! WRONG BARREL. ANYBODY FANCY A GHERKIN?

It was inevitable that a queen as young and glamorous as Mary would attract nutcases who got fixated on her. One of these was the Earl of Arran, son of the Duke of Chaterherault. In fact, back in France, when she'd been newly widowed, he was one of the men whose names had come up as possible husbands. Mary had turned him down, but Arran, who had several screws loose, was obsessed with her. He told people his secret plans of kidnapping her and getting her in a situation where she would have been forced to marry him. (If you were raped in those days it was considered that you had been completely dishonoured and usually meant you had to marry your rapist to restore *your* reputation!)

Arran claimed that it wasn't his idea, but Bothwell's, and both of them had to appear before the Queen's Council. In the end, Bothwell escaped from Edinburgh Castle and skipped the country, but Arran, who was now completely bonkers, was shut up for the rest of his life.

A couple of years later, Mary had another stalker.

MARY'S SECRET DIARY

January 1563

Something of a fright last night. Fortunately it shows that the palace guard is doing its job. When they searched my bed-chamber before I retired for the night, they found young Chatêlard hiding under my bed. I knew the poor boy was in love with me, of course, but I had no idea he would do something so stupid. Imagine what could have happened if they hadn't found him!

Chatêlard was a young French poet. Mary liked him and was friendly with him, but she never considered him boyfriend material – he wasn't nearly grand enough. She let him off this time, but Chatêlard gave her another surprise – on Valentine's Day.

MARY'S SECRET DIARY

14 February 1563

Chatêlard has done it again! After I'd told him he was not to come into my presence on pain of death! Today, as I was just getting undressed, he came hurtling into the room and fell at my feet. I had no one in attendance, but two of my ladies. We screamed - all of us,

> I think, and Moray was in the room within seconds, his dagger ready. By this time, Chatêlard was on his knees, clutching at my robe and telling me that he only wanted to apologize. But who knows? I cannot pardon him again. He is to go for trial at St Andrews next week.

Chatêlard was hanged a week and a day later. In the meantime, he had made a statement that he was agent for the French Protestants, and part of a plot to damage Mary's reputation. But then on the scaffold, he cried out:

> *Adieu, the most beautiful and cruel princess in the world.*

When Mary had problems like this, John Knox had a field day. He said it was all Mary's fault for leading Chatêlard on.

> MARY FLEMING CAN SLEEP IN MY BED FROM NOW ON — THERE'S SAFETY IN NUMBERS. BUT THE SOONER I GET A HUSBAND TO LOOK AFTER ME THE BETTER.

Looking for Mr Right

Ever since she'd been widowed, Mary had been keeping her eye out for a suitable husband. The trouble was, everyone had an opinion about whom she should marry.

77

Queen Elizabeth was famous for playing games about who she would marry, but Mary was almost as good at leading suitors on. Mary had Lord William Maitland tootling all over Europe, doing deals and spinning yarns. She also had her cousin Liz quite worried.

79

Meanwhile, Mary was getting pretty annoyed at Liz's own marriage plans – especially when Liz then offered Mary one of Catherine de Medici's younger sons, who'd been in nappies when Mary was growing up at the French court.

MARY'S SECRET DIARY

December 1564

I don't believe it! Not only does it look as if cousin Liz is going to marry Charles, she has sent the French ambassador to the English court to offer me his little brother Anjou. Talk about second best. As if I would marry him! I made no bones about it to the ambassador. I said, 'Grandeur for grandeur, I prefer the Prince of Spain.'

In fact, Mary could have done a lot worse. Charles IX of France died young and the Duke of Anjou became Henry III of France. So if Mary had married him, she would soon have been Queen of France once more, which would have been one in the eye for both Catherine de Medici and cousin Liz. And she would also have saved herself a whole heap of trouble. However – she didn't.

MARY'S SECRET DIARY

January 1565

The French marriages are both off, and so is the Spanish. I know who to blame. The truth is no one wants to get on the wrong side of my cousin Liz. No matter

> how young and beautiful I am, they all see me as a liability. What to do? I think, I shall forget about getting married, and go and have a holiday. They say there is very good hunting in Fife this year.

Enter Henry, Lord Darnley

It was while Mary was away on her hunting trip in Fife that she met her second hopeless husband – Henry, Lord Darnley. It wasn't their first meeting. When Mary had been newly widowed, his mum, who was dead ambitious, had packed young Henry (aged 16) off to France, hoping that Mary would fall in love with him. There was nothing doing that time, but this time when they met Darnley was 19, and Mary was feeling unloved and unwanted by all the eligible princes of Europe, and she liked the look of Darnley...

> *He is the lustiest and best-proportioned lang man that I have ever seen.*

When Mary used the word lusty she meant good-looking, and when she said lang, she meant tall.

Who was he? Well, just look at his family tree.

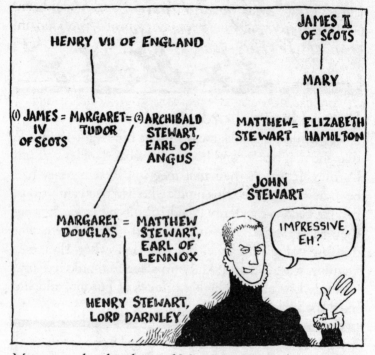

Mum was the daughter of Mary's gran, Margaret Tudor, and her second husband, Archibald Stewart, Earl of Angus (the one who had kidnapped James V). This made her the half-sister of James V and the niece of Henry VIII, and therefore someone else with a claim to the English throne.

Dad's great-grandmother was the daughter of James II, which gave him a claim to the Scottish throne.

In other words, Darnley was of Scottish royal blood – and he also had an excellent claim to the English throne – especially as he was Catholic and a lot of Catholics thought Elizabeth was illegitimate.

Darnley's dad had been kicked out of Scotland in 1543 for supporting Henry VIII, and Darnley had been brought up in England. Darnley came to Scotland in 1565 with Elizabeth's permission. According to Sir James Melville, he was…

> More like a woman than a man; lusty, beardless and baby-faced.

Darnley was a bad lad, into wine and women big time. He was also selfish and weak, but none of this showed up on Mary's radar screen. She saw a gorgeous guy who knew how to behave in royal circles, and was a lot more civilized – at least on the outside – than many of her Scottish nobles.

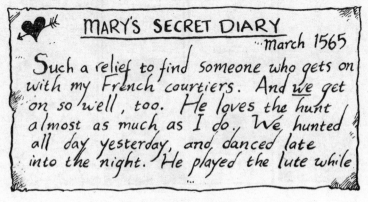

MARY'S SECRET DIARY

March 1565

Such a relief to find someone who gets on with my French courtiers. And we get on so well, too. He loves the hunt almost as much as I do. We hunted all day yesterday, and danced late into the night. He played the lute while

I sang. He is such a gentleman, he complimented me on my dancing and my voice, and gazed into my eyes with such feeling. Is he in love with me? I think he is... and I cannot believe my luck. I have found the perfect husband. As if his looks and character were not enough, we are also cousins. Together our claim to the English throne will be unbeatable. And it is so much more sensible to keep these things in the family. A foreign prince would only complicate matters. Oh bliss! I am in love!

What did other people make of Darnley?

CATHERINE DE MEDICI

GETS HER OUT OF MY HAIR.

THE CARDINAL OF LORRAINE (MARY'S UNCLE CHARLES)

THE BOY IS A COMPLETE *⊙☆℥*⊚!*

* NAUGHTY FRENCH WORD

LORD MORAY

IF SHE MARRIES THAT LOSER AND HAS A BUNCH OF KIDS, BANG GOES MY CLAIM TO THE THRONE!

LIZ

SHE CAN'T MARRY WITHOUT MY PERMISSION! IT AFFECTS THE ENGLISH SUCCESSION!

Who knows what Liz really thought about the marriage? She always hated her courtiers marrying, especially if it strengthened their claim to the throne. On the other hand, it seems odd that she allowed Darnley to go to Scotland when he did. Maybe she thought that he would distract Mary from other, more powerful suitors. Or maybe she was even more devious. Maybe she knew what a loser Darnley was, and this was her way of shafting Mary good and proper. Look what her own ambassador said:

A greater plague to her there cannot be; a greater benefit to the Queen of England's Majesty could not have been chanced.

Darnley was all charm until he was sure Mary was in love with him; then his attitude changed and, even before the wedding, he became inconsiderate and rude. Mary rushed on, ignoring the warning signs. She was going to marry her beloved lang man, come what may. She had to get permission from the Pope (because she and Darnley were cousins and so weren't supposed to marry under Church Law) and also from Elizabeth (because she and Darnley both had a good claim to the English throne, so their children would have a *very* strong claim). Mary did the right thing and sent off letters to the Pope and cousin Liz, but she didn't bother to wait for the replies.

Mary was full of the joys of spring. She and her servants even dressed up (or rather, down) as ordinary townswomen and went through the streets of Edinburgh collecting money to give a party for her servants.

Elizabeth, meanwhile, was beside herself with fury when she received the letter from Mary. The first thing she did, not being able to lock up Darnley himself, was lock up his mother. The Countess of Lennox was sent to the Tower of London. Then Sir Nicholas Throckmorton was sent riding up the Great North Road.

GO AND FETCH HIM BACK!

BUT... SIR NICHOLAS! COME BACK! THE QUEEN HAS CHANGED HER MIND!

SCOTLAND ←

TELL HER IF SHE MARRIES DARNLEY, THERE'S NO CHANCE OF HER SUCCEEDING TO THE ENGLISH THRONE. BUT IF SHE MARRIES ROB DUDLEY, I MIGHT JUST CONSIDER IT...

I WISH SHE'D MAKE HER MIND UP.

SCOTLAND: HOME OF THE HAGGIS

The row about the marriage went on and on like a thunderstorm. Mary's brother, Moray, was dead against it. He didn't want Mary having children, and he was afraid that once she had a husband, Mary would no longer turn to him for advice. All this opposition just made Mary more determined than ever. She started giving Darnley titles to make him sound grand enough to marry a queen.

MARY'S SECRET DIARY

7th July 1565

There are rumours that my brother Moray has been seen in England at the Court of the Queen. That he is seeking arms and men to overthrow me and prevent my marriage. Truly, I was wrong ever to trust him. He was only good to me as a means to his own power. He thought me a weak woman, and that he could continue to rule Scotland as he had done after my mama's death.

He will not stop me marrying. And neither will my cousin, who wants me to play her game, and turn down every suitor. What good will that do, when there is an heir neither to the throne of England nor to the throne of Scotland?

H and I will marry secretly in two days time. That way no one can prevent the wedding.

We don't know if Mary really did have a secret wedding on 9 July, but the English ambassador wrote to Elizabeth telling her she had. He also said that Darnley had been seen in the streets of Edinburgh with a tall, red-headed boy, who was probably Mary dressed as a feller.

YOU MAKE A MOST CONVINCING MAN, YOUR MAJESTY.

I *AM* A MAN, YOU IDIOT! THE QUEEN'S THE ONE IN THE HAT.

Mary's official wedding did not take place until the 29 July – and before then, Mary bestowed a few more titles on Darnley.

HER MAJESTY IS PLEASED TO ANNOUNCE ON THIS, THE 23RD DAY OF THE SEVENTH MONTH OF THE YEAR OF OUR LORD FIFTEEN HUNDRED AND SIXTY-FIVE, THAT SHE HAS GRACIOUSLY BESTOWED UPON HENRY DARNLEY THE TITLE OF DUKE OF ALBANY...

OH MY! HE'S GOT HIS AIN WAY THEN...

JUST SO LONG AS WE DINNAE HAVE TO CALL HIM KING O' SCOTS.

Next, Mary had the banns proclaimed in St Giles Cathedral. The banns are an announcement of a forthcoming marriage – they're called so that if anyone knows a reason why you shouldn't marry (like your being married to someone else, for example) they can come forward and say so. Mary was going to marry Darnley within days, but before she did, there was one more thing she had to do. Five days later it was announced...

The reason Mary gave Darnley this series of quick promotions was that she was sensitive about marrying beneath her. Darnley might have had royal blood in his veins, but her first husband had actually actually been king of one of the most powerful countries in Europe. Darnley just wasn't in that league.

The wedding itself was a bit of come-down the second time around as well, though Mary did her best.

THE SCOTTISH HERALD

30 July 1565

QUEEN O' SCOTS WEDS

Beautiful young widow Mary Queen of Scots arrived at St Giles Cathedral at six o' the morn yesterday to marry the love of her life, Henry Darnley, Earl of Ross, Duke of Albany and – as of yesterday – King o' Scots. The couple exchanged rings, and knelt in prayer. Then the herald called out 'God Save the King' – but the only voice that called back 'God save His Grace' was the groom's father, the Earl of Lennox.

The marriage service was conducted according to Roman Catholic rites. However, the new King did not stay for the Mass that followed. A source close to the royal couple suggested that the new King, whose father is a Protestant, thought it wiser not to partake of the Roman Mass at a time when feelings are strong about the religion of the Queen. He rejoined his wife later for a lavish wedding breakfast, after

91

which gold and silver coins were thrown to the crowd.

The celebrations continued all day, with only a brief rest in the afternoon before supper and dancing.

John Knox made no secret of the fact that he was not pleased. He does not like the marriage, and he found the celebrations offensive, especially the dancing.

The wedding was over. The marriage was public. Now it was time to sort out Mary's brother, Moray, who had come back from England with a troop of men to fight Mary. He didn't stand a chance. The Scottish nobles might not like having a young queen who had made her arrogant young husband their king, but the ordinary people adored her. People loved a royal wedding as much then as they do now. They thought a beautiful young girl deserved a chance of happiness. The people of Edinburgh rose in support of her, and Moray and his pals were driven out of Scotland.

Now all Mary had to contend with was her new husband.

MARRY IN HASTE, REPENT AT LEISURE

Mary was madly in love with Darnley when she married him. Six months later she couldn't stand him. What went wrong?

Basically, now Darnley had got what he wanted, he behaved as if he wasn't married at all. He went out drinking and womanizing. As if that wasn't hurtful enough, he was rude to her in public as well.

MARY'S SECRET DIARY

December 1565

I don't know what I have done to make him so vile to me. He seems not to want to know me now I am pregnant. He goes out all the time and will not tell me where he is going. I had hoped he might help me rule this difficult country, but he takes no interest. Gone are the days when we would dance all evening, and he would play his lute while I sang. He has used me to get power and position, there is no mistaking it.

I do not know whether to be glad or sorry that I am Queen, and have people around me all the time. It is hard, knowing that they know how he is with me. But they are so kind to me, my French and Italian servants especially. They are not part of the Scottish family feuds and are loyal only to me. David Riccio especially. I know I can trust him with my most secret secrets. He is such a capable man, with a beautiful singing voice. Now it is Riccio with whom I sing in the evenings. A shame - for him — that he is such a hunched and ugly man.

A brutal killing

David Riccio was Italian, but his official position was French Secretary. This meant that he took care of Mary's French correspondence – and that he knew what she was saying to all her French relations. Maitland – who was Mary's official secretary – didn't, and he resented it. Plenty of other nobles resented Riccio's power too, because anyone who wanted to speak to Mary had to go via Riccio, and this meant a bribe. And Darnley, who thought everyone else behaved the way he did, didn't like him either. He was jealous of him and Mary – even though there was nothing to be jealous of.

Soon everyone was muttering and plotting with everyone else. Lord James Stewart, Earl of Moray, in exile down in England, was in on the plot. So was Darnley. The idea was to seize Riccio and put him on trial – but things got out of hand.

THE SCOTTISH HERALD

10 March 1566

MURDERED BEFORE HER EYES

The Queen's secretary, David Riccio, was stabbed to death yesterday as the horrified Queen of Scots looked on helplessly.

The Queen, who is seven months pregnant, was dining with Riccio and three or four other courtiers when King Henry entered the room via a back staircase. The Queen

invited him to sit beside her but before the King could do so, a gang of armed men burst into the room. Led by Lord Ruthven, they said they had come to take Riccio away. Eyewitnesses said that Riccio tried to hide behind the Queen, but the men seized him. In the scuffle that followed he received 56 stab wounds. When the physician got there, he was already dead.

The news reached the town, and by the early hours a crowd had gathered outside Holyrood Palace, armed with spears and pikes and demanding to see the Queen. King Henry came out to speak to them, and told them to go home, that both he and the queen were safe.

This morning King Henry issued a proclamation saying that the Estates, who had assembled to hear the charge of rebellion against Lord James Stewart, Earl of Moray, had been sent home indefinitely. There has been no sign of the Queen, who is rumoured to be a prisoner.

MARY'S SECRET DIARY

10 March 1566

I am captive, and, Riccio is dead. I will never hear that beautiful, voice again. I have, lost a good friend.

It happened so fast and it was so confusing, but I must write down what I remember, for one day it may come to court, and I must be clear on the facts. At dinner — myself, my sister Jean, my brother Robert, Arthur Erskine and Riccio. We had no sooner begun our meal than Darnley came up the back stairs, drunk and belligerent. As we made him welcome, there were clanking sounds from the back stairs, and into the room, in full armour, came Lord Ruthven, pale as a ghost.

'I have come to take the Italian away,' he said. And then he spoke to Darnley, in a way that made me wonder if my husband was in league with him.

I stepped between Ruthven and, poor Riccio as Robert and Arthur drew their swords, to defend me. But then more armed men came running up the stairs, a candle fell, and next thing, I knew, Andrew Ker of Fawdonside was prodding my pregnant belly with his pistol.

Then George Douglas drew Darnley's dagger and leant past me to knife Riccio — so close I felt the coldness of the steel. They all fell on him like frenzied animals, and when he was dead, they threw him down the stairs.

As this was going on, Darnley was whining at me that it was all my fault, that I had broken my promise to give him an equal share in the running of the kingdom. My temper snapped and I told him that the fault was his (because of his behaviour) not mine, and that henceforward I would lie with him no more.

Then Ruthven, who is a sick man, begged leave to sit and called for a cup of wine. I turned on him and told him that if, from the shock of this night, I died in childbirth and the kingdom lost its queen, then the King of Spain and my uncles Guise and Lorraine, yea and the Pope himself, would take revenge on him and his heirs.

And then I was kept in my bedchamber, with guards on the door. Yet even so, there came a message from my Lords Bothwell and Huntly who, learning there was something ill afoot but finding themselves outnumbered, planned to escape to fight another day. They asked me if I wished to come with them, but I said no, that the Queen of Scots would remain in her palace. And so I remained in my room all night, pacing the floor while my vile and traitorous husband slept drunkenly in his own chamber.

ZZZZ
HIC
ZZZZ

Moray and his pals were due back in town that week because they were to be tried for rebellion. (Liz had been agitating for this for some time.) He timed his arrival so that it looked as if he couldn't possibly be involved in the plot, but so that he was just in time to reap the benefits. When he went to see Mary, he made out that he was absolutely disgusted by what had happened. Maybe he was. Moray wanted his power back, but he hadn't expected things to get so messy and violent. When he met Mary, she put her arms round him and told him that if he had been there, they wouldn't have treated her so roughly.

MARY'S SECRET DIARY

11 March 1566

My brother swears he knew nothing of the plot. Doubt this is true, but I need his help. I told him that it was all Darnley's fault that he and the other Protestant lords have been kept so long from home. It is true. Darnley is jealous of anyone he thinks is close to me. My brother pretended that now he is happy with my marriage, and helped me make up my quarrel with Darnley. I played along, because I must escape. I have persuaded them that I think I am about to miscarry – God, forgive me and protect me from so doing – and they, Moray and the others, have agreed to make Darnley my keeper on their behalf. He, poor fool, was full of remorse when he sobered up, and swears he will do everything in his power to help me. So the plan is set. Not a soul except my French servants within this palace knows what is going on. I durst not write it here for fear that someone find it...

Darnley was about to betray his fellow-conspirators. That night, at midnight, he and Mary slipped out of a back door of the palace.

Henry and Mary on the run

101

It took seven hours to ride from Edinburgh to Dunbar, where there was a castle loyal to Mary. It was morning by the time she arrived. She was starving. She ate a big breakfast of eggs and then she sat down to write some letters telling everyone her version of what had happened.

Meanwhile back in Edinburgh…

It wasn't long before nobles and men loyal to Mary heard what had happened and came flocking to Dunbar to support her cause. Only a week after the murder of Riccio, the attempted coup was over.

THE SCOTTISH HERALD

18 March 1566

WELCOME BACK, MA'AM

The citizens of Edinburgh turned out in force today to welcome back the Queen to her capital city. The Queen of Scots, heavily pregnant, but looking well after her ordeal, rode triumphantly into Edinburgh at the head of a force of 8,000 men. At her side was the Earl of Bothwell, warden of Dunbar castle since last week, when he proved his loyalty to the Queen.

Since the terrible night when her secretary was stabbed to death in front of her eyes, the Queen has astonished everyone by her strength and decisiveness. Last week she announced that she would pardon everyone not directly involved with the murder. As a result, half the plotters have fled the country, while the other half are keen to prove their loyalty.

The Queen declined to return to Holyrood, and is instead lodging in Edinburgh Castle.

Mary, of course, suspected that Darnley and Moray were involved in the murder of Riccio. Nevertheless...

HER MAJESTY THE QUEEN OF SCOTS WISHES IT TO BE KNOWN ON THIS, THE 21st DAY OF MARCH IN THE FIFTEEN HUNDRED AND SIXTY-SIXTH YEAR OF OUR LORD, THAT SHE IS PERSUADED OF THE INNOCENCE OF HER HUSBAND KING HENRY IN THE MATTER OF THE MURDER OF HER SECRETARY, DAVID RICCIO.

THAT'S NICE THEN.

However, the other conspirators weren't having that...

APRIL 1566

YOUR MAJESTY
PLEASE FIND ENCLOSED THE BOND TO WHICH
YOUR HUSBAND PUT HIS SIGNATURE. IF YOU
READ IT YOU WILL SEE THAT HE WAS A
PRIME MOVER IN THE PLOT TO KILL DAVID
RICCIO.

A WELL-WISHER

Mary had guessed it all along, but there wasn't much she
could do about it. She was about to give birth, and for the
moment she turned her attention to making all the
necessary arrangements. In those days, childbirth was a
dangerous business. Mary knew that she might not survive
it, and if she died, Scotland would be without a queen.

MARY'S SECRET DIARY

May 1566

Somehow, I have to free myself of
Darnley, but how? Too many other
things to think about for the moment.
Have made a will, saying who is to
have all my jewellery — this in the event
that the baby dies with me. If not, he
or she is to have the lot.

Have been generous to Darnley and
his family, but that's just to make up
for the fact that he is most definitely
not on the council which will rule the

country, if I die. Have named Bothwell for that. He has been loyal both to me and to Mama. He is a strong man, and understands the Scottish nobles far better than I do myself. I would have done far better, to have married him instead of the horrible HD.

Will think about how I can get rid of HD after I have had the baby. In the meantime, I have invited my brother and Argyll to remain in the castle with me as my 'guests'. They are better where I can keep an eye on them than free to wander the country making trouble while I am out of action.

12 July 1566

My dear cousin,

This is to let you know how pleased I am that you have overcome your little setback with the Scottish nobles. What an unpredictable bunch they are, I must say. Though, of course, your difficulties are no more than my own might have been had I been so unwise as to marry one of my own subjects. There is a great deal to be said for staying single, my dear.

However, too late for that, you must be thinking, as you approach your time. Please know that I am thinking of you and praying for the swift and easy delivery of a fine son.

I remain, your loving cousin,

Elizabeth

Mary was hoping for a swift and easy delivery too. As she went into labour, she had a whole lot of Catholic relics paraded through the room to invoke the help of God and his saints. And just to be on the safe side she went in for some 'alternative' help as well. The Countess of Atholl, who practised witchcraft, cast a spell so the pain of Mary's birth pangs would by shared by Lady Reres, who got into bed beside Mary and writhed with pain along with her. It didn't do much good. Mary had a long miserable labour – but at the end of it, she produced a healthy baby boy. She sent for Darnley to show off the child to him.

Messengers were sent to England straight away – to Queen Liz, inviting her to be the baby's godmother, and to his gran, the Countess of Lennox, who was still a prisoner in the Tower of London.

Mary was out and about quite soon after the birth of her baby. Royal mums didn't look after their own babies. Little Prince James was sent off to Stirling Castle, with his nanny and wet nurse, Lady Reres, while Mary went hunting in Fife once more, where she had met Darnley. He wasn't invited along this time.

One husband too many

Mary was still thinking about how she could get free of Darnley. Basically, the only two options were divorce or death. She was worried that divorce might put a question mark over her son's legitimacy. (In Catholic law, the most usual grounds for divorce were that you should never have got married in the first place because you were too closely related – which would make your children illegitimate.) If James were illegitimate, then bang went his right to succeed to any throne, English or Scottish. So divorce was out. It looked as if the only way out for Mary was for Darnley to meet with a nasty accident.

At this stage no one quite knows what Mary's relationship was with Bothwell. He had supported her after the murder of Riccio, and she had made him Warden of Dunbar Castle. Darnley hated him and so did Moray, but then Moray was jealous of anyone he thought had more influence than him with the Queen. Mary had come to depend on Bothwell, and he was a bit of a hunk. Some people thought she was falling in love.

MARY'S SECRET DIARY

october 1566

I don't know why I find him so attractive. He's short, he's not good-looking – though there is something rather sexy about that battered nose – and worst of all he's Protestant. And married. I don't want to make another mistake like I made with Darnley. But he's always there for me. And it's not just because I'm young, beautiful and Queen of Scots, because he was loyal to Mama as well.

I'm not the only one who finds him attractive. There was that Norwegian girlfriend (Anna something) when he first came to court. And they say he was bewitched so that he fell in love with a 61-year-old when he was 24. And loads of others.

He would make a strong king. But I must stop thinking like this. He is Protestant and married, and much shorter than me, and not grand enough, and I am married, anyway.

But I do like him.

Bothwell's nose was battered because he was always getting into fights. He had been a prisoner in the Tower of London *and* in Edinburgh Castle. And now he got into a fight with a border raider from England. Mary was at Jedburgh when she heard that Bothwell was lying wounded at his house, the Hermitage, 30 miles away. Together with her brother, Moray, and a train of servants, she rode there and back in a day to see him. Sixty miles in the saddle was a hard day's ride, even for a hardened horseman.

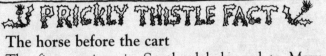

The horse before the cart

The first carriage in Scotland belonged to Mary Queen of Scots and was brought over from France. The roads in Scotland were really terrible, however, so carriages weren't much use. Mary herself generally preferred riding. She could ride thirty miles in a day, no problem, and once, when she was on the run, rode ninety miles without stopping.

When Mary fell ill a short time later, some people said it was because of her marathon ride to see Bothwell. Others said her illness was all down to stress. Mary could see no way out of her marriage to Darnley, who went on pestering her and stirring up trouble wherever he could. It may even have been that someone had tried to poison her, for she was violently sick. For a few days it looked as if she wouldn't recover. Mary herself thought she was going to die, and summoned all her nobles to her bedside. She told them that, whatever happened, Darnley was not to inherit the crown. It was to go to her baby son, James. Then she went into a coma.

And while she lay between life and death, my lord of Moray shewed his true colours, rifling through her jewel boxes and pocketing the best pieces.

Mary recovered consciousness, and as she got a little better, was taken by litter to Edinburgh. When she met Huntly and Maitland, she was very public about her loathing for Darnley, and how she wished to be rid of him.

WHAT AM I TO DO? I CANNOT DIVORCE HIM.

DON'T WORRY MADAM, SOME OTHER WAY WILL BE FOUND. I'M SURE LORD MORAY WILL LOOK THE OTHER WAY.

GOOD. JUST SO LONG AS IT DOESN'T STAIN MY HONOUR OR MY CONSCIENCE.

Did Mary want to be free of Darnley simply because he was a pain in the neck, or was it that she wanted to marry someone else? And was that someone else the Earl of Bothwell? Historians have argued about it down the years. We'll never know. What we do know was that many people saw how unhappy she was at this time. The French ambassador said...

The royal christening was coming up, so Mary put a brave face on it. The Scottish Parliament, the Estates, had put up money towards the expenses but it wasn't nearly enough for the sort of posh christening Mary had in mind. She ended up buying new outfits for all the nobles, so that they wouldn't let the side down in front of her French rellies. The nobles hardly recognized themselves.

THE SCOTTISH HERALD

18 December 1566

PAPISH PRELATE SPRINKLES PRINCE

There was nothing private about the way the Queen practised her religion yesterday when she had her six-month-old son baptized at Stirling Castle.

Catholic prelates, garbed in costly vestments, led the torch-lit procession between rows of courtiers. Crowds of foreign courtiers attended the ceremony. The Comte of Brienne represented the King of France and carried the baby prince, swathed in lace and brocade, into the chapel. Numerous Scottish Catholics followed, carrying all the paraphernalia of a Catholic christening.

The baby's godmother is Queen Elizabeth of England. She was unable to attend, but sent a solid gold font weighing 28 pounds. She was represented at the christening by Queen Mary's half-sister, Jean, Countess of Argyll, who held the baby during the ceremony.

Many home-grown Protestant nobles stood outside the chapel, unable to stomach the Papish rite. Others stayed away altogether. Also missing was Henry, King of Scots. No explanation was given for his absence, although he was said to be staying in Stirling Castle at the time.

Afterwards there were masques and dancing. The Estates had voted a massive £12,000 to fund the pageantry. Many thought it a waste of money.

The Herald asks if this was wise. Do we really want our money spent on aping the sort of fun and fripperies that go on at the French court?

Darnley went flouncing off to Glasgow immediately after the christening. He was angry that everyone could see he was not in favour with Mary, and had a head full of schemes to overthrow her and rule on behalf of their son. Mary heard these rumours, and moved Prince James from Stirling Castle to Edinburgh just in case. She was still dithering about whether she could get a divorce without messing up James's claim to be legitimate.

Meanwhile – anything for a quiet life – she had pardoned all the plotters who had done down Riccio. The Earl of Morton now returned to Scotland.

Then, suddenly, Darnley fell ill with a horrible disease. Mary, sent her doctor to see him, and eventually went over to Glasgow herself to visit him.

MARY'S SECRET DIARY
January 1567

His poor face is all covered in blisters. I feel quite sorry for him, his good looks all gone, and feeling so ill, poor love. And he was pathetically pleased to see me. Now he is unable to go out drinking, and he is quite repentant, and mild-mannered, I almost remember what it was I saw in him. He has agreed to come back to Edinburgh with me. I think he still hopes for a reconciliation, but my plan is to have him where I can better keep an eye on him. And if, when he recovers, his behaviour mends, who knows?

Darnley didn't altogether trust Mary. He refused to go to Craigmillar Castle, where she wanted to put him, and instead took up lodgings in a house called Kirk O' Field which had belonged to the Lord Provost of Edinburgh. Mary furnished it for him, and slept in a small bedroom beneath Darnley's. All seemed quiet and harmonious between the King and Queen. Until…

THE SCOTTISH HERALD

20 February 1567

KING FOUND DEAD

All Edinburgh was woken last night as a massive explosion rocked the city. As people rose from their beds, they found the house called Kirk O' Field, where King Henry had been staying, razed to the ground. Rescuers were desperately searching by lamplight for survivors, pulling at the rubble with their bare hands, when a ghoulish, blackened figure appeared on the city wall. It was King Henry's manservant, Nelson, who had been thrown clear in the explosion.

He was the only survivor. Two blackened corpses were dug from the rubble and by morning the Earl of Bothwell, Sheriff of Edinburgh, announced that the king's body and that of his page had also been found a little way from the house.

The Queen was said to be in deep shock. It was only by chance that she herself had not been sleeping in the house. She had left there at 10 yesterday evening to attend a masque to celebrate the wedding of one of her French servants, Bastien Pages.

Who done it?

That was the question everyone was asking, and a lot of people were answering it too. Anonymous placards began appearing all over Edinburgh.

The English ambassador sent a sketch of the scene of the crime to Elizabeth's chief minister, Sir William Cecil.

February 1567

Dear William,

Please find enclosed a map of the scene of the crime, with bodies.

Darnley was in his nightgown; his servant carried a cloak. It seems that they realized something was afoot and made their escape, lowering themselves from the bedroom window by rope on to a chair in the garden below before the house exploded, but someone saw them, and despatched them without mercy. The rope marks on their necks suggest they'd been strangled.

As to who is responsible, rumours abound, but I have reliable information that Sir James Balfour purchased £60 worth of gunpowder in the week leading up to the explosion.

The big question, of course, is: why gunpowder when they are all so handy with their knives this side of the border? It only makes sense if the plan was to kill the Queen as well — and she herself seems to think that the plot was aimed at her.

All the best,
William Drury

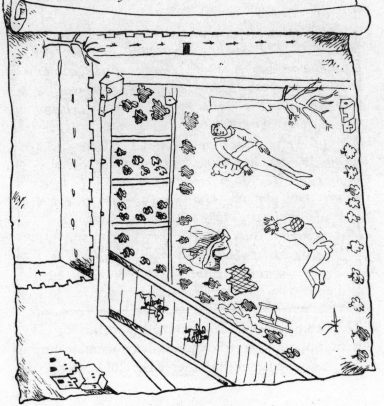

Mary behaved very strangely after the murder. She ordered the court into mourning but she didn't behave like a grieving widow. Instead, she went to weddings, she hunted, and generally behaved as if she didn't care. A bit suspicious, you might think. Unless, of course, she was trying to prove to the plotters that they didn't scare her.

MARY'S SECRET DIARY

February 1567

They meant to kill me, but I will show them that I am not feart of them. I must be seen in public so that all know I am safe.

Bothwell swears he had no hand in it. This I doubt, though I am as certain as I can be in this treacherous country that he meant my own person no harm. No, it is Morton, Moray, Balfour and the others that I do not trust.

If Bothwell does have Henry's blood on his hands, then that is a matter for him and his God. I had no part in it, though, God forgive me, I am relieved to be free of such a dastardly husband. I think that the Scottish people too must know, in their hearts, that it is for the best.

The Scottish people didn't know any such thing. They were shocked to see the Queen living it up, instead of grieving at home for the father of her child. Most people thought Bothwell was the chief murderer, and it stuck in their throats to see him riding around Edinburgh investigating the crime and punishing people for placarding. They thought the whole thing stank of hypocrisy and corruption.

In fact, Mary was pretty miserable at this time. Elizabeth sent a new messenger to see her with a letter of condolence.

> *She received me in a dark chamber, so I could not see her face, but by her very words she did seem very doleful, and did accept my sovereign's letters and messages in a very thankful manner...*

Because there had been no real effort to investigate the crime, Darnley's father, the Earl of Lennox, was beside himself.

15 March 1567

Your Majesty,

As the grieving father of a beloved son, your husband, the late King Henry of Scots, I humbly seek leave of you to bring a private prosecution before the Estates against the Earl of Bothwell for his murder.

I remain your loyal subject,

Lennox

24th March 1567

Dear Father-in-law,
Of course you may bring a private prosecution. In fact, the date has been set for 12th April. Just don't bring all your men with you — it would be a recipe for civil war. I suggest you bring a small retinue of no more than six men.

Mary

Lennox knew there were at least 4,000 of Bothwell's supporters in Edinburgh. He had been planning to come with 3,000 of his own men, and he certainly wasn't stupid enough to come without them. He stayed away and the trial went ahead without him. This was exactly what Bothwell had hoped for.

THE SCOTTISH HERALD

13 April 1567

BOTHWELL GETS OFF

Not guilty. That was the verdict of the Parliament after a trial lasting seven hours.

It was a big day for the Earl of Bothwell. He rode to Parliament at noon in his best gear, with the Earl of Morton and Sir William Maitland by his side. As he passed Holyrood House, the Queen could be glimpsed watching the procession, with her lady-in-waiting, Mary Fleming (who married Sir William in January) at her side.

Did the Queen know that a messenger had arrived from the English court at 6 a.m. that morning? A source who refused to be named said that he was carrying a letter from the English queen, requesting that the trial be postponed till the Earl of Lennox could be present to put his case against Bothwell. It is thought that the Queen was not told of the messenger's arrival – but even if she had been, would she have stopped the trial?

Bothwell was in high spirits as he left the court.

'You see? I'm clean as a whistle!' he told his supporters. 'I did not kill Henry Darnley. And I'll personally knock the head off anyone who says different.' For good measure, he paid a crier to go around the city telling everyone this news.

The ordinary folk of Edinburgh were not convinced – nor were they intimidated by Bothwell's threat of violence. A fresh crop of placards sprung up around the city:

WHAE D'YE THINK YE'RE KIDDING, JIMMY?

q. Who makes life go with a BANG? A. JAMES HEPBURN, EARL OF BOTHWELL.

BOTHWELL DOES BLACK DEEDS, PUTS THE QUEEN IN WIDOW'S WEEDS, SHOWS HIS SWORD AROUND THE TOWN, NEXT WE'LL SEE HER IN A WEDDING GOWN.

HE PACKED THE PARLIAMENT WI' PALS, TO CLEAR HIS MURKY NAME. HE THINKS HE'S GOT AWAY WI' IT, BUT FOLKS KNOW HE'S TO BLAME.

He packed the hoose wi' dynamite To blow the king sky high. The Queen she stayed away that night, You have to wonder why.

A few days later Mary rode to Parliament with Bothwell beside her carrying her sceptre, the Duke of Argyll carrying the crown, and Crawford carrying the sword of state. The Estates were to be asked to confirm the verdict of the court which had tried Bothwell. They did so. That night he was cock-a-hoop. He was in the clear. And he knew exactly what he needed to do next.

AND ANOTHER HOPELESS HUSBAND

The night Bothwell was acquitted he was out on the town with his cronies as well as a few other people he wanted on his side. He wasn't just celebrating. He wanted their signatures on a document.

The Ainslie Tavern Bond

Seeing how James Hepburn, Earl of Bothwell, is completely innocent of all the evil deeds of which he has been accused, and Parliament has agreed he is innocent, and seeing how the Queen is destitute of a husband, and for all our sakes cannot be allowed to remain single, we would like to support the said James Bothwell in his generous offer to become her next husband, always supposing she fancies a hearty, affectionate chap like ~~myself~~ BOTHWELL

We, the undersigned are 100 per cent behind this generous offer, which we suggest the Queen takes up before some foreign prince gets his paws on her.

Argyll ~~Seton~~ Glencairn Maitland

CASSILIS Sinclair Atholl

Huntly MORTON Sutherland

All Bothwell's dinner guests, who were full of drink by this time, put their names to this Bond – nine earls, eight bishops and seven barons among them. Perhaps it was something to do with all his henchmen standing around fingering their daggers.

Then, next day, Bothwell took Maitland and another courtier with him for support and went to visit Mary to tell her the good news.

MARY'S SECRET DIARY

20 April 1567

The cheek of it! As if I could possibly marry him after all that has happened! The whole country thinks he murdered Henry. The fact that the rest of them are all in it up to their necks as well, is neither here nor there. I told him point blank that it was out of the question. Apart from anything else, he's not long married. What about his poor wife?

And yet Maitland is right when he says that the country needs a strong ruler, and there is no doubting Bothwell's loyalty. Or his strength. If I could marry him, it might be a good solution. But it's out of the question, so that's that.

Tomorrow, I ride to Stirling, to see darling little James. He is ten months old already. What a lot has happened in that time!

Kidnapped!?!

Mary spent the day in Stirling, playing with baby James. The following day she was taken violently ill with stomach pains on the journey home, and had to rest in a cottage near Linlithgow. She was well enough to continue the next day and just outside Edinburgh she found Bothwell waiting for her with a troop of 800 men. He said he had come to warn her that there was trouble in Edinburgh, and that it wasn't safe for her to enter the city. He told her he would take her to Dunbar.

No one believed him. Some of Mary's bodyguard were ready to fight, but Mary told them that the odds were stacked too heavily against them, and she didn't want an unnecessary bloodbath. She allowed Bothwell to lead her horse on byways around Edinburgh and then across open country the 40 miles to Dunbar. One of her servants managed to slip away to warn the Provost of Edinburgh.

THE SCOTTISH HERALD

24 April 1567

QUEEN ABDUCTED!

The alarm bells of Edinburgh were rung last night, summoning all able-bodied men of the city to arms, as news reached the city that the Queen had been abducted by the Earl of Bothwell.

James Borthwick, who had been travelling with the Queen, reported that the Earl of Bothwell waylaid Her Majesty at the Bridge of Almond. The Queen's retinue was greatly outnumbered, and the Queen agreed to accompany the Earl to Dunbar.

It is not clear why the Earl, who is on good terms with the Queen, found it necessary to abduct her, but last night fears were being expressed for the Queen's safety.

MARY'S SECRET DIARY
26 April 1567
Well. He's done it now. I have no choice but to marry him.

Sir James Melville declared, 'The Queen could not but marry him, seeing that he had ravished her and lain with her against her will.' However, the English ambassador, William Drury, said that, 'While the manner of her seizure may seem to have been forcible, it was known to have been otherwise.'

In other words, Drury thought the kidnap was a put-up job and Mary went along with it because it let her off the hook. It's very hard to know whether this is true or not. But whatever her true feelings, Bothwell was divorced from his wife within days. They arrived back in Edinburgh together, on 6 May.

AYE, BUT IS SHE HIS CAPTIVE OR HIS QUEEN? HE'S LEADING HER BY THE BRIDLE!

The one thing you could be absolutely certain of in sixteenth-century Scotland was that if you were winning in the power game, then everyone else would gang up on you. Bothwell was no exception. It was time for ANOTHER bond.

The Stirling Bond

We the undersigned do solemnly swear that we will liberate our Queen of Scots from her captivity to the Earl of Bothwell, and restore her to power. To this end we will invite the Earl of Moray to return from England, and seek help from the Queen of England and the King of France.

Signed, this 1st day of May 1567

Atholl   Argyll   MORTON.

PS: The Ainslie Tavern Bond was a mistake. We never really signed it.

Another hasty wedding

Bothwell pressed ahead with the wedding. Orders were given for the banns to be read, announcing the marriage. The Dean of St Giles, however, who was a pal of John Knox, wasn't having it.

I WILL NO READ THESE BANNS TILL I HAVE IT IN WRITING FROM THE QUEEN THAT I AM TO DO SO. FURTHERMORE, I ACCUSE BOTHWELL OF BREAKING THE LAW OF THE KIRK, OF ADULTERY AND OF RAVISHING. I AM SUSPICIOUS OF COLLUSION BETWEEN HIM AND HIS WIFE, THE SUDDEN DIVORCEMENT AND PROCLAIMING WITHIN FOUR DAYS; AND LAST I SUSPECT HIM OF THE KING'S DEATH, WHICH THE MARRIAGE WILL CONFIRM...

WHAT? JUST WAIT! I'LL SEE HIM HANGED!

It didn't stop the wedding. In fact, at this point it seemed that nothing could stop Bothwell. By 12 May Mary had made him Duke of Orkney. She had knighted many of his henchmen and pardoned everyone who signed the Ainslie Tavern Bond. (She could hardly go on being cross with them, seeing as she was going to marry Bothwell.) Three days later – and only 12 days after Bothwell's divorce – Mary and Bothwell were married.

Some of Mary's French servants had been with her since her arrival in France. They were loyal to Mary, but they weren't too happy about what was going on.

131

AYE, BUT IT WAS A SAD WEE CEREMONY THE DAY, AS THEY SAY IN THIS COUNTRY. SO VERY DIFFERENT FROM HER OTHER WEDDINGS. IN THE FIRST PLACE IT WAS A PROTESTANT CEREMONY, WHICH YOU WILL KNOW DID GRIEVE MY LADY VERY SORE.

AND IN THE SECOND, IT WAS A DRAB OCCASION. MY LADY WORE NO FINERY, AND HER WEDDING GIFT TO THE EARL, OR RATHER THE KING AS I SUPPOSE WE MUST NOW CALL THE LITTLE THUG, WAS JUST A PIECE OF OLD CIVET FOR HIS GOWN.

WHEN I THINK OF THE SPLENDOUR AND PAGEANTRY OF HER FIRST WEDDING, AND EVEN THE SECOND (WHICH GOD KNOWS, WAS ILL-ADVISED). THERE WAS NO JOY AT ALL, AND BY EVENING THE QUEEN AND HER NEW HUSBAND WERE SCREAMING INSULTS AT EACH OTHER.

OVERNIGHT MORE OF THOSE TERRIBLE PLACARDS APPEARED ON THE STREETS SO THAT BY MORNING I THINK SHE WAS IN DANGER OF COMPOUNDING ALL HER SINS BY TAKING HER OWN LIFE. SHE WAS HEARD CALLING FOR A KNIFE THAT SHE MIGHT KILL HERSELF, AND MORE THAN ONCE HAS THREATENED TO DROWN HERSELF.

133

If she really believed that it would work out somehow when she married Bothwell, she was soon to see how wrong she was.

MARY'S SECRET DIARY
may 1567

The people of Edinburgh hate me and, worse, my Church has abandoned me. Though I told my confessor that I repented my sins — in particular the sin of marrying in the Protestant religion — the Pope has made it clear that he wishes to have no more to do with me. I suppose I should be grateful that I am not to be excommunicated, although I cannot even be sure of that.

As for Bothwell, he is as vile and rude as Henry. The only difference is that he is civil to me in public, even keeping his head uncovered. But behind closed doors his temper is unspeakable. He insists I must give up golf, cards, dancing, hunting, and singing.

I am lost. Moreover, brother Moray is back in Scotland, and mustering an army. What is to happen to me?

On the run

By the end of May, just five weeks after Bothwell had kidnapped her, Mary was so unpopular in Edinburgh, that she and Bothwell both had to leave the city. They went to Borthwick Castle, hoping to muster an army from among Bothwell's border supporters, but Borthwick was surrounded, and Mary had to escape dressed as a man.

MARY'S SECRET DIARY
12 June 1567

Met up with Bothwell again, and rode for Dunbar. Here we are safer, but I have no clothes except the doublet and hose I have ridden in all day. I have borrowed a dress from a townswoman, very unfashionable, with a red petticoat which does not fit.

That I am come to this!

By mid-June, Mary and Bothwell waited with a small army on Carberry Hill near Edinburgh, hoping for reinforcements. The rebel lords gathered on the opposite side of the valley. It was a long, hot day. Neither side wished to attack because it meant losing the high ground.

Various options were put forward:

1 The French ambassador offered Mary a deal: if she abandoned Bothwell, the rebels would come over to her side. She refused.

2 It was suggested that Bothwell could fight one of them in single combat. Bothwell agreed, Mary refused.

Meanwhile the reinforcements did not arrive and, worse, half of Mary's troops were going over to the enemy. Now the rebels offered again: ditch Bothwell, and come over to us. Mary agreed, provided Bothwell was allowed to escape. The lords agreed to this. They didn't want Bothwell hanging around. He might bring up all the ways they'd been involved in Darnley's murder and everything else.

So Bothwell scarpered, but not before he'd pressed into Mary's tired and sweaty hands a copy of yet ANOTHER, earlier bond – the Craigmillar Bond, which all the nobles had signed way back when they promised to get rid of Darnley. This was proof that Morton, Moray, Maitland, and most of the other Scottish nobles had been involved in Darnley's murder.

Mary had surrendered, thinking that she would still be treated as queen. She was badly mistaken.

Mary was kept prisoner in the Provost's house that night. Despite being heavily guarded, she managed to get a letter to Sir James Balfour who was holding Edinburgh Castle, but next morning she was desperate and was seen at the window, shouting for help.

She was kept in the Provost's house a few days. The rebels had hoped that she would divorce Bothwell, but she refused to do so. Now they didn't know what to do with her. Finally they took her to Holyrood – but not for long. When she'd eaten a meal, they brought her outside, where horses were waiting. She was going to Stirling, they told her, to be reunited with baby James.

But they were not going to Stirling. Mary was going to Lochleven Castle, which stands on an island in the middle of Loch Leven. She would be imprisoned there for nine months. She was just 24 years old.

A SCOTTISH ALCATRAZ

Mary was imprisoned in Lochleven Castle in the middle of a deep loch near Perth. The Protestant lords knew it would be difficult for anyone to rescue her from there.

They also knew that the people who lived there wouldn't want her to escape. They were:

Sir William Douglas was related to most of Mary's current enemies (he was Moray's half-brother and Morton's cousin). His mum, Lady Margaret, was a tough old bird, who in her day had been a girlfriend of Mary's dad and was none other than Lord James Stewart, Earl of Moray's mum. (She didn't like Mary because she felt her son should be king.) Pretty Geordie was William's brother and Margaret's youngest son. (He soon fell helplessly in love with Mary.)

No one had told Lady Margaret, who was the big boss of Lochleven Castle, that Mary was coming, so nothing was ready. However, they didn't have to worry too much, because Mary was past caring by this time. She was completely shattered by all she had been through, and lay on her bed refusing to speak or eat for two whole weeks.

When she came to, Lindsay and Ruthven (son of the sick man who had taken part in Riccio's murder) had some news for her.

MARY'S SECRET DIARY

June 1567

They have told me that they will only consider releasing me if I divorce Bothwell. I told them it was out of the question. Do they think I am no better than them, changing my loyalty with every change of my fortune?

What they do not know is that I am pregnant. (At least, I think that is the reason my monthlies have not come.) Even if I wished to divorce Bothwell, where would that leave the baby? Besides, Bothwell is my only hope. He may be a rough diamond, but diamond he is compared to the others.

Now that they knew that Mary wouldn't ditch Bothwell, the lords felt they had the perfect excuse for keeping her locked up. On the 16 June 1567 it was declared…

IN THAT SHE DID NOT PURSUE HER HUSBAND'S MURDERER, BUT RATHER MARRIED HIM, THE LORDS HAVE DECREED THAT SHE BE KEPT PRISONER INDEFINITELY. AND IN THAT THE EARL OF BOTHWELL HAS NOT GIVEN HIMSELF UP, HE IS DECLARED AN OUTLAW AND HIS ESTATES ARE FORFEIT. SIGNED, THE EARLS OF MORTON, GLENCAIRN AND HUME.

There was something very mucky about the fact that the earls who said Mary was guilty of murder were the very same earls who had been part of the murder plot themselves, and who had signed the Ainslie Tavern Bond suggesting that Mary marry Bothwell. They made matters worse by disposing of everything she owned as if she was dead.

Liz, mean as she was, outbid Catherine for Mary's famous pearls, and the rest of Mary's jewellery was sold to bidders from all over Europe. Her private chapels were dismantled and the Catholic trappings destroyed and even her clothes were given away by one of her Italian servants.

MARY'S SECRET DIARY
July 1567

They say they are keeping me here till I see sense about Bothwell, when they will restore me to my proper place. But any fool can see that they never mean to release me. That is why they keep me here so far from Edinburgh. Bothwell is outlawed, and all his men are being hunted down and murdered. They now want me to abdicate and agree to the coronation of baby James. I have refused. How long will it be till they finish me off?

Mary wasn't the only person worried about this. The English ambassador to Scotland, Sir Nicholas Throckmorton, who liked Mary, was also worried. He wasn't allowed to see her, but he did manage to get a letter to her hidden in a scabbard. And pretty soon, he got a letter back.

18 July 1567

Dear Nick,
Yes, things are pretty grim. The old lady, as Lady Margaret is called by everyone, is very severe. I do not trust either Ruthven or Lindsay, and it is no exaggeration to say that I am, every day, in fear of poison or dagger. The only

light in the darkness is Pretty Geordie, a handsome youth, who pities me, I think. I pray you bring to bear what pressure you can. I remain your loyal friend,

Mary

At this point, Elizabeth decided to get in on the act.

YOU CAN TELL THEM THAT THIS IS NO WAY TO TREAT A CROWNED QUEEN, MY LORD AMBASSADOR. IF THEY CAN'T DEAL WITH HER, THEN I'M VERY HAPPY TO TAKE OVER.

I'M NOT SURE THAT'S QUITE THE WAY THEY WANT TO PLAY IT.

ALSO, I THINK IT WOULD BE MUCH BETTER IF BABY JAMES WAS BROUGHT UP IN ENGLAND, AWAY FROM ALL THOSE ROUGH MEN. HIS GRANDMOTHER CAN LOOK AFTER HIM.

BUT ISN'T SHE STILL A PRISONER IN THE TOWER?

SO WHAT? I CAN SOON CHANGE THAT.

PLENTY OF OTHER CHILDREN HAVE BEEN BROUGHT UP IN THE TOWER.

Forced to abdicate

In the middle of July, Mary had a miscarriage. She had been expecting twins and Bothwell was the father. She bled heavily and was very pale and weak when Lord Lindsay and another lord appeared with a new document, and told her to sign *or else*.

ARTICLES OF ABDICATION

I, Mary, formerly known as Queen of Scots, do resign the crown to my infant son, Prince James, on the grounds that I am so vexed and broken and unquieted by the responsibility of queenship that I can carry on no longer.

I name my brother, James, Earl of Moray, as regent. I agree that the Earl of Morton and his mates should join with Moray to form a government.

At first Mary, weak and ill though she was, refused to sign. Lindsay told her he would drag her from the house if she didn't, at which Pretty Geordie leapt to her defence, and called on the castle servants to defend her.

MARY'S SECRET DIARY
July 1567

I signed in the end. What else could I do? But all the while I was shouting, so that everyone could hear that I was only doing it because I was forced to and that such a signature was worthless before the law.

Geordie is a good friend, although he is not a wise man. Lindsay will

---

145

not forget. Already he has had his revenge on me. I am to be housed in the keep across the yard from the main house — away from Geordie and the family.

I am going to get out of here, and then I'll show them!

THE SCOTTISH HERALD

30 July 1567

LONG LIVE THE KING!

For the third time running, Scotland has an infant monarch. Yesterday, amid widespread rejoicing, little Prince James, just a year old, was crowned King of Scots in Stirling Parish Church. The Earl of Morton swore the oath of kingship on the child's behalf, and John Knox preached the sermon.

Bonfires were lit across the country – over 1,000 fires were counted in Edinburgh alone.

'We'll get on a lot better wi' a Protestant king,' said Mistress Annie Mackay, a fishwife of 49. 'This is what we've been needing, a fresh start. Let's just hope he disnae go the same way as his mother.

146

MARY'S SECRET DIARY

30 July 1567

I couldn't make out what on earth was going on last night. Sir William was dancing and singing in the castle garden. When I asked him at supper for what reason he was so merry, at first he would not tell me. Then, a few minutes later, he asked me why I was not celebrating too. I asked him what I had to celebrate, and he replied, 'Why, the coronation of the new king.' I dropped my spoon and screamed out, quite without thinking. The rest of the evening I spent in my room, weeping. I am a crowned queen, anointed before God. How dare they cast me aside! May God avenge this wrong that has been done me.

It was a bad summer for Mary. She became very ill from the stress of everything that had happened. Yet even as Moray took over as regent, and things seemed to be settling down, opposition to the Protestant lords was starting to build. The Hamiltons, old enemies of Morton and the Douglases, had not been invited to the coronation. They had been lying low, but they could see a use for Mary. And Mary herself was trying to sort out her situation.

October 1567

Dear Cousin Liz,
Sorry not to have written to you before this, but things have been a bit difficult. I know you know this, but perhaps you don't know just exactly how bad it's been. My clothes - or some of them - have only just caught up with me, and this letter will have to be smuggled out, at great personal risk, by one of my ladies-in-waiting.

I know that you will be outraged that I have been treated so badly. I am therefore asking you, please, to, send English troops. A few hundred will do, because I know my own people well enough. When they see that, I am in with a chance once more, they will rise to my defence.

Some indication of when the troops can be expected would be most useful to my allies here.

Thanking you in anticipation, I remain your most loving and devoted cousin,
Mary

Mary wrote a letter in much the same vein to her ex-mother-in-law Catherine de Medici. There was no reply from either queen, and no troops either, so Mary decided to take matters into her own hands.

MARY'S SECRET DIARY

26 March 1568

Oh, how frustrating! So near and yet so far. Yesterday I dressed up as a washerwoman and managed to get halfway across the loch. But the boatman was looking at me very strangely, and suddenly he said, 'Ye have very white hands for a washerwoman, madam.' And my eyes met his, as I waited for what he would say next. 'And ye're a very tall lady too,' he went on. 'It wouldn't be the Queen herself I'm rowing, would it?'

'Some say I am not the Queen,' I replied. 'Pray do not take me back.' For already he was turning the boat back towards the island.

'I can do nought else if I value my life,' he said. 'But dinnae fear, I willnae tell a soul.'

Yet, as Geordie said to me, maybe it is for the best. For it needs men and weapons on the other side.

Mary on the run again

Within a month a new rumour was circulating at the Scottish and English courts. Mary had asked Pretty Geordie to marry her! Moray wasn't having that. He didn't want his sister flirting with her gaolers. Geordie was ordered off the island.

149

MARY'S SECRET DIARY
April 1568

Moray has fallen for it! The plan has worked! So, now Geordie can sort things out on the mainland, while his little cousin Willie helps me here. I have given him one of my pearl earrings which he is to send to me when it is safe for me to make my escape.

The other piece of good news is that Maitland has sent me a ring! It shows a lion tied up and a mouse gnawing at its bonds. It can only mean one thing – he is back on my side, and preparations are afoot to spring me, from this dreadful gaol. I knew I only had to sit and wait for the lords to fall out among themselves.

On 1 May that year, Willie Douglas, Geordie's orphan cousin who was staying with the family, organized a May Day masque. It was a long day, and Mary went for a rest in the late afternoon.

I WONDER WHAT WAS GOING ON TODAY? THERE WAS A WHOLE BUNCH OF HORSEMEN GATHERED IN KINROSS WHEN I WAS OVER THERE...

151

THE BOAT ROWED TO THE MAINLAND WITH MARY HIDDEN UNDER A SEAT...

GEORDIE AND LORD SETON WERE WAITING ON THE SHORE...

I MADE IT! I MADE IT!

HOORAY! IT'S THE QUEEN, DISGUISED AS A SERVANT!

NO, I REALLY AM A SERVANT. THE QUEEN'S STILL UNDER THE SEAT...

AS SHE RODE TOWARDS SETON'S PALACE AT NIDDRY, PEOPLE CAME OUT OF THEIR HOUSES TO WATCH AND CHEER...

THERE! I KNEW THEY STILL LOVED ME!

That night Mary's pen never stopped. She wrote letters to everyone she could think of, telling them she was back in the game. And she sent a messenger to Denmark, where Bothwell had fetched up in prison, asking that he be released. (Bothwell had been captured in Norway by some old mates of his ex-girlfriend. They passed him on to the King of Denmark, who thought the husband of the Queen of Scots might come in handy one day when he was negotiating with somebody or other, and kept him in prison.)

Next day she wanted to ride to Dumbarton Castle, which was a good choice for two reasons.

1 There were people there loyal to her who had been holding out since Carberry.
2 She could take a ship for France if things didn't work out.

However, although Mary was out of prison, she still wasn't her own woman. The men who had come to meet her were Hamiltons. They saw her as a pawn in their struggle against Moray and Morton. They suggested she went to the town of Hamilton, where she signed a document revoking her abdication.

Now the Hamiltons told Mary that she hadn't a hope of getting her kingdom back unless she won it in battle. So, instead of heading for Edinburgh, Mary went south towards Glasgow. Moray had been caught on the hop by her escape, but he wasn't long in gathering an army. He met her at Langside. He had only half as many troops as Mary, but Mary's men were more interested in fighting each other. Mary was so desperate that she rode on to the battlefield herself to try and get them all going in the right direction. It was hopeless. Within hours, Mary was on the run, south towards Galloway. With her was a small band of supporters led by Lord Herries.

MARY'S SECRET DIARY

May 1568

What a time I have had. Since the battle, we have ridden over 90 miles through the wild Glenkens, without stopping. The horses were exhausted, and so were we. When we did stop, there was nowhere to sleep but on the ground – thank goodness for heather – and nothing but oatmeal to eat. This morning we crossed the Dee at Tongland, and Herries and his men blew up the bridge to prevent any who might be following. A good woman came forth from a croft and gave us a bowl of milk. It had been standing all night and it was sour, but it was food, and I forced some past my lips. Herries says he will grant the woman and her family the right to live in her croft rent-free, for ever, in gratitude for her help.

Mary went in the direction of Dumfries, and then doubled-back to Dundrennan Abbey. She had made up her mind to take a ship to England.

MARY'S SECRET DIARY

May 1568

Herries tells me that I should sail for France. He argues that I have lands there, and friends, and could live comfortably until the time is right to mount an attack on Moray. He says that the Queen of England is no friend of mine, and that I know no one there, having no relations except Darnley's mum, who hates my guts. But I am tired, and for all I know my cousin's ships will intercept me in my flight. Then I will be her prisoner, and who knows what she may do. She could even send me back to Moray. If I land in England of my own free will, then I am her guest, and courtesy demands that she invite me to court. When we meet then I know I can win her over.

Were these the reasons Mary decided to go to England? Or was it one of the following reasons – what do you think?

- She was too proud to go back among her French relations as a defeated queen.
- It seemed easier to mount a counter-attack from the north of England than from France and she thought the Catholic lords in England – many of whom lived in the north – might rise up and help her win back her throne.
- She was too stressed out to make a sensible decision.
- She'd had too much wine that night.

I'VE DONE FOR SCOTLAND. LET'S SEE IF I CAN DO FOR ENGLAND TOO!

She may even have decided that she'd had such a hard time ruling her own kingdom, she'd come to England so she could make life as difficult as possible for cousin Liz. We'll never know. Whatever the reason, Mary set sail for England, and it turned out to be the worst decision of her life.

Mary was 25 years old when she landed in England. Luckily for her, she didn't know that she would be a prisoner till the day she died, 19 years later. Mary, up till then, had had one of the most eventful, exciting, glamorous lives ever, not to mention scary and unhappy thanks to those hopeless husbands. From now on she would find that time slowed to a crawl. She was an ex-queen with no power and no influence.

It took her a long time to realize this. To start with, things went quite well.

MARY'S SECRET DIARY

27 May 1568

I knew I was right to come here. People are so kind. The haberdasher with whom I lodged the first few nights offered me a bolt of cloth so that I can have some new clothes, (I am a pretty sorry sight — all that riding through gorse and

158

brambles). And a lovely man called Richard Lowther arrived with an escort of 400 horse to bring me here to Workington. He provided horses for me and my party out of his own pocket. When my fortunes are better I will see he is well rewarded.

Workington was the home of Sir Henry Curwen, a pal of Lord Herries. He'd been told Herries was looking for a temporary home for a young Scottish heiress, who might make a good bride for Curwen's son.

We don't know if Sir Henry Curwen was taken in by this description of Mary, but he said yes anyway.

The people of Cumberland who saw the tall, beautiful woman guessed at once who she was. Soon the place was buzzing with the news and gossip.

159

The news soon reached London that the Scottish Queen had landed in England. There was consternation. Mary was a danger to Elizabeth because many Catholics thought she had a better claim to the English throne than Liz herself. Although Liz toyed with the idea of bringing her cousin to court, she soon thought better of it. Mary was kept where she was – a long way from London. She was allowed to keep 40 servants, and to go out for walks or to watch football matches, provided she was accompanied by a bodyguard of 100 men.

MARY'S SECRET DIARY

June 1568

...they are there supposedly to protect me, but actually, of course, it is to stop me escaping. Or being rescued by well-wishers. Meanwhile, I am as short of clothes as ever. I asked my cousin Liz if she could spare me a few of hers – she is almost as tall as I am – but the dresses she has sent are a sorry collection, shabby, ill-fitting and not at all becoming. Perhaps she doesn't wear nice clothes. Perhaps these belonged to one of her waiting-women.

My hair is a mess. It grows shaggier by the day, and I sorely miss my beloved Mary Seton, who always knew how to keep it looking nice.

Elizabeth sent Sir Francis Knollys up to 'look after' Mary. He went back to tell Liz all about her. Like many men before him, he'd fallen under her spell. He thought her an impressive woman with…

…*an eloquent tongue and a discreet head, stout courage and a liberal heart.*

REALLY? TELL HER WE CANNOT POSSIBLY RECEIVE HER AT COURT UNTIL HER NAME HAS BEEN CLEARED OF HER HUSBAND'S MURDER.

Mary was livid when she got the message. She knew that the very people who were accusing her were all party to the murder of Darnley. She started writing letters.

June 1568

Dear Cousin Liz,
Thank you for your message. However, I should like to point out that it was at your request and against my own better judgement that I allowed the earls who now accuse me to return from exile in England. In the light

> *of this,, I think you bear some responsibility for the position in which I now find myself.*
>
> *Your loving cousin,*
>
> *mary*

Mary wrote letters to lots of other people too. Catherine de Medici, the Duke of Anjou, the Cardinal of Lorraine all received more or less the same letter saying…

1 She was innocent.

2 She was broke.

3 Please could they send her some money.

No one in France was too sympathetic. They thought she'd made a complete hash of things and they certainly weren't rushing to send her money. And Queen Elizabeth was not best pleased when she heard Mary had written to her French rellies.

TELL HER THAT IF SHE APPEALS TO FRANCE FOR HELP, THEN SHE WILL HAVE ENGLAND FOR AN ENEMY!

Liz had now latched on big-time to the idea of England arbitrating in the row between Mary and her nobles. She had Mary moved south to Bolton, which was further from the border, and sent Lord Herries with a message.

SHE SAYS THAT YOU MUST SUBMIT TO A TRIAL. HOWEVER, SHE WILL RESTORE YOUR THRONE WHATEVER THE OUTCOME. THOUGH IF YOU'RE FOUND GUILTY, THE LORDS WILL NOT BE PUNISHED FOR THEIR REBELLION.

I'M **NOT GUILTY!**

Moray was nearly as angry as Mary at the idea of the English Queen getting mixed up with Scottish affairs. That was until Liz's chief minister, William Cecil, had a word with one of his pals.

YOU CAN TELL LORD MORAY THAT THE QUEEN HAS ABSOLUTELY NO INTENTION OF RESTORING THE SCOTS' QUEEN TO HER THRONE.

OF COURSE, IT WOULD HELP HER A GREAT DEAL IF THE SCOTS' QUEEN WERE TO BE PROVED GUILTY OF MURDER.

Moray got Elizabeth's drift. He decided he was happy to go along with her plan...

Mary's first trial – York 1568

This was a real put-up job. Elizabeth had no right to try Mary in the first place, and the trial itself was rigged to make it impossible for Mary to clear her name. Mary wasn't allowed to appear, and her own commissioners were half-hearted about defending her.

To make sure the court found her guilty, Moray suddenly 'remembered' a silver casket of letters which he claimed he'd found on one of Bothwell's supporters the previous year. When the Duke of Norfolk, who was heading the inquiry, read the letters, he told Queen Elizabeth that it would be impossible

to find Mary 'Not Guilty'. These were supposed to be letters from Mary which proved that Bothwell had been her boyfriend when Darnley was still alive, and, even worse, that she had plotted with Bothwell to kill Darnley.

But were they genuine? Probably not. Most people today think that they were forgeries, maybe based on letters from one of Bothwell's (many) other girlfriends. They were copied out by hand for the court, and then returned to Moray. There were no forensic tests in those days, and after they went back to Moray they disappeared and have never been seen from that day to this. But the appearance of the casket letters helped Moray's case against Mary, so it was very convenient.

Meanwhile, Mary was fighting back with the only weapon she had – her sex appeal. With a bit of help from Lord Maitland, the Duke of Norfolk (the one heading the judicial inquiry) got it into his head that marriage to Mary would strengthen his claim to the English throne.

When Cecil told Liz she was incandescent with rage. She took Norfolk off the inquiry and had him shut up in the Tower of London. Then she moved the inquiry to London – but made Mary stay up north.

MARY'S SECRET DIARY
November 1568

It is so unfair. Yesterday I heard that my brother Moray is never out of Liz's company. She hears his side of the story but not mine. I have sent a letter to her telling her that I will order my commissioners to boycott the inquiry unless I, too, am allowed to speak to her.

Mary hadn't got the point. She was in no position to boycott anything. Elizabeth didn't want Mary attending the court, because she knew she would deny that the Casket letters were anything to do with her – and that people would probably believe her. If her commissioners stayed away too, so much the better.

Gradually it came home to Mary that she hadn't a hope. She sent a message to the Spanish ambassador in

166

London, telling him that the Catholic nobles of northern England were gathering in her support, and if Philip of Spain sent an army, she would be Queen of England in three months and ready to marry anyone he wanted.

Philip did not rush to support Mary. He knew that it was by no means certain she would be Queen of England in three months. A few days after she sent that message, the English inquiry brought in its verdict – or rather, its non-verdict.

THE SCOTTISH HERALD

11 January 1569

NOT PROVEN!

This was the verdict of the English court on Mary, ex-Queen of Scots.

After months of argy-bargy, in which the Scots' Queen was not even allowed to see the main evidence against her, the Sassenachs* decided that she was not guilty of the murder of her husband – but that she was not innocent either. However, the English Queen has taken it upon herself to decide that our queen is not fit to rule.

If Mary is not guilty, then it follows that someone else is,

* Sassenach is the Scottish word for English.

but that this the last verdict the bossy English Queen wants to see. Placards around the time of the murder pointed the finger at the Earl of Bothwell, but no one thinks he acted alone. Rumours persist that some of the men who hold high positions in the land today were implicated in Darnley's murder. The English Queen chooses not to see that – in fact, she has sent Moray home with a handsome £5,000 in his pocket.

The fact is that this case should never have been tried in England. We Scots are perfectly capable of running our own affairs. We don't need England to act as judge, jury and gaoler.

Plenty of Scottish people felt like that. On the other hand, many of them believed that Mary was a murderer, and that she shouldn't be queen. John Knox was thrilled to see the back of her. Now he had a Protestant regent again while Mary was safely locked up in England.

YIPPEE.

STEADY NOW, JOHN. DON'T GET CARRIED AWAY.

Prisons and plots

By this time, it was blindingly obvious that Elizabeth was no friend of Mary's. Mary was not a guest but a prisoner, and right away she was moved to a new, more secure prison – Tutbury Castle, in Staffordshire.

It was a bitterly cold February and Mary had a terrible journey.

MARY'S SECRET DIARY
February 1569

I thought I was going to die. It was so cold, all the ruts in the road were frozen hard, and stayed frozen all day. Mary Livingstone took ill and had to be left behind. Then poor Knollys had tidings that his wife had died, and was very cast down. I myself collapsed just outside Rotherham. It started as a terrible cold, but I think the strain of my situation made it worse, and our little procession had to rest up for several days. Then we were told Tutbury was not ready and, to make for Sheffield, but we found out that all the furnishings had been sent to Tutbury! Now we are here and it is ghastly. A huge, ugly fortress on a hill in the middle of a marsh. Drafts such as I have never known, and as for the loos...

At least the Shrewsburys seem a pleasant pair, though he is obviously very under her thumb.

Liz was giving Mary a change of prison because news had reached her that her gaoler Knollys, like other gaolers before him, was falling for Mary. Mary was put in the hands of the Earl and Countess of Shrewsbury.

The Earl of Shrewsbury
a.k.a. George Talbot
Filthy rich and very mean. Other than that he was OK. He quite liked Mary, and thought she should inherit the English throne.

The Countess of Shrewsbury
a.k.a. Bess of Hardwicke
She was 49 and on her fourth husband. (She'd had eight children with her second.) She was that rare thing in Elizabethan England – a career woman. She bought and sold

land, lent money, built houses, and married her children off to her stepchildren through her subsequent husbands to keep all the dosh in the family.

During her time with the Shrewsburys Mary was allowed to hunt and walk, and she and Bess sat and sewed and gossiped together for hours on end. You can see the results of their work at Hardwicke Hall, the house that Bess built in Derbyshire. The Shrewsburys hated Tutbury too, and moved Mary to other houses of theirs when they could get away with it.

170

But whichever house she was in, Mary was a prisoner. She couldn't do what she wanted. Here are the conditions that the Earl of Shrewsbury laid down for Mary.

To Mr Beton,
Master of the Household to the Queen of Scots.

1 All the Queen's people shall leave the Queen's apartments for their own lodgings at 9 p.m., winter and summer, and remain there until 6 a.m. the following morning.

2 None of the Queen's people may wear a sword, either in the house, or when Her Grace is out riding.

3 None of the Queen's people may carry bows or arrows at any time, neither to the field nor to the butts.

4 None of the Queen's people may go outside the castle without my special permission, and if they do, they may not come back in either to the castle or the town.

5 You or your deputy must inform me or one of my officers if Her Grace wishes to go for a walk.

6 In the event of an alarm sounding, none of the Queen's people may come forth, either from the castle or their lodgings. And if they do come out, then they will be put to death.

At Sheffield, the 26th day of April, per me,

SHREWSBURIE

All in all it was a very restricted life for Mary and her servants. She was cut off from everyone – from her French relations, from her son James, and from Bothwell (who was still in prison in Denmark).

~PRICKLY THISTLE FACT~

Learning the language

In the sixteenth century, Scots was a completely different language from English. When Mary was a prisoner in England, she had to learn to speak and write English. Her first letter in English went like this:

Excuse my ivel vreitn thes furst tym.

Mary spent her days dreaming up schemes for getting out of prison and for getting her revenge on everyone who had injured and insulted her.

One possibility was to take yet another horrible husband – in other words, marry her way out. Liz had released the Duke of Norfolk from the Tower by this time, and Mary thought he was her best chance.

July 1569

My Norfolk,
I cannot tell you how happy your letter has made me. And as for the diamond, it is so beautiful! It sparkles like a light in my darkness. Thank you, my dear man.
Considering how little I know you,

I feel so very close to you. If only circumstances were different, and we might meet as free people, unencumbered. Little happens here. I long for release. Your news is so welcome. Please write again.
Your loving friend **mary**

Dear Moray,
                                                    July 1569
As you may or may not know, your sister and I have become increasingly close, and I write to enquire how you would view the possibility of seeking the dissolution of her marriage to the Earl of Bothwell. From what I hear, he forced her into marriage, and I feel that this might allow grounds for the marriage to be dissolved. I make no secret of the fact that I desire her freedom so that I myself may marry her, with a view to uniting our two kingdoms in the future.
Yours sincerely,
Norfolk.

                                                    July 1569

Dear Norfolk,
I have never heard of such an outrageous idea. She disposed of one husband to enable her to marry another, and now he no longer suits, she wants to dispose of him! Out of the question.
Yours disgustedly,
Moray

This response from Moray was a bit much. After all, he had locked up Mary in Lochleven Castle precisely because she had refused to divorce Bothwell. However, it was hardly a surprise. The last thing Moray wanted was his sister marrying into the English nobility. She might fight back for her own crown, and maybe even bring about a union between England and Scotland ... and where would that leave him?

Marriage between Mary and Norfolk was the last thing Elizabeth wanted, too. Apart from the fact that she was dead set against any of her courtiers marrying, and often clapped them in the Tower if they did, Norfolk was in touch with the Catholics in the north who wanted to rescue Mary and make her Queen of England in Liz's place.

NORFOLK, I HEAR YOU HAVE A LADY LOVE. MARRIAGE PLANS, EVEN.

WHO, ME? NO, NOT ME, MA'AM. DEFINITELY NOT ME.

DON'T LIE TO ME! I KNOW YOU'RE PLANNING TO MARRY THE SCOTTISH WITCH AND PUT HER ON MY THRONE!

Norfolk ended up in the Tower again, which kept him out of harm's way as the northern Catholics marched north to free Mary. Elizabeth had her moved to

Coventry Castle just in case, but the rebellion fell apart very quickly. Liz was safe once more.

17 December 1569

Dearest Cousin,
I am so glad that you have overcome those wicked rebels. I just want you to know that I had absolutely nothing to do with them. I would not dream of doing anything that would bring unrest to your kingdom.
I wish you a long life and great happiness.
Your cousin, Mary

Elizabeth wasn't convinced. Her own Privy Council had just voted to recognize Mary as heir to the throne of England. And Mary was still writing to Norfolk.

January 1570

My Norfolk,
I hate to think of you shut up in the Tower because of me. If it helps, know that I am ready to live and die with you.
Your loving friend Mary

Norfolk was flattered by Mary's attention. He liked the idea of rescuing Mary. So when Elizabeth let him out of gaol, he began plotting with the Duke of Alva. The plot that Norfolk got involved with became known as the Ridolfi Plot, after an Italian messenger who got caught with incriminating letters on him. This time, there were no more chances for Norfolk. He was tried and sentenced to death. He was executed in 1572 – the first execution of Elizabeth's reign.

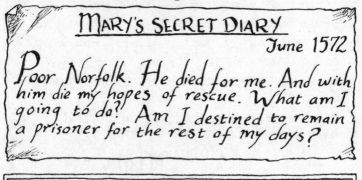

MARY'S SECRET DIARY

June 1572

Poor Norfolk. He died for me. And with him die my hopes of rescue. What am I going to do? Am I destined to remain a prisoner for the rest of my days?

News from abroad

In Scotland, it was business as usual … Maitland and Moray had fallen out, and in 1570 Moray was shot dead in the street by John Hamilton of Bothwellhaugh, who had a long-standing grudge against him.

AND I DIDN'T EVEN ASK HIM TO DO IT! GIVE THAT MAN A PENSION FOR LIFE!

Lennox (Mary's father-in-law) became regent, though he was opposed by Maitland. Lennox died during a raid on Stirling Castle in 1571.

Soon it was the turn of the Earl of Morton to be regent.

He persecuted Catholics, forced Edinburgh Castle to surrender and hanged the man who had been holding it for Mary all this time.

Meanwhile, in France, there was a famous massacre on St Bartholomew's Night in 1572, when Catholics went on the rampage and killed hundreds of Huguenots (French Protestants).

This didn't do Mary any good, because it made the English Protestants very nervy about their Catholic neighbours – and the Scottish Queen who might be their rallying point.

By 1574, Mary had had enough. She decided to make Elizabeth a sensible offer.

February 1574

Dearest Cousin,

I hope this letter finds you in good health. I am well-treated by the Earl and his wife, although he complains something rotten about the expense of keeping me. So, knowing that a large part of this expense comes from your pocket, dear cousin, I would like to propose a way of saving you money. Why not allow me to return to my lands in France? I will bother no one there, and live out my life quietly as mistress of my French estates. The weather is so much better there, it would ease my rheumatism.

Wishing you all the best, your loving cousin Mary

P.S. Of course, restoring me to my Scottish lands would also get me out of your hair, if you felt inclined to help me...

Why did Mary add the postscript? It's just possible that Liz might have agreed to ship Mary back to France, if she'd been convinced that Mary had no more ambition to rule. As it was, Elizabeth saw red.

It wasn't even as if Liz had shown any signs of being nice to Mary. Just after Moray died, Mary had sent two ponies to her son James, complete with bridles and saddles. They never arrived. Liz put a stop to it. However, although she refused to let Mary disappear to France, she did agree that Mary could spend a few weeks at Buxton Spa, which was just a few miles from Shrewsbury. There were hot springs there, and it was quite a social place, so every summer for quite a few years Mary had a change of scene and new people to talk to. Most of the year, though, it was hunting and sewing with Bess.

One year, there was an earthquake which damaged Sheffield Castle and gave Mary a terrible fright.

Her room was sunk from the shock of it. I was more afraid that she would fall than that she would escape.

In that same year, 1575, Mary made a wonderful red petticoat for Elizabeth.

May 1575

Dear cousin Mary,
Thank you so much for the petticoat. I am most impressed by the needlework – it must have taken you hours. Glad to hear the rheumatism is a little better.
Your loving cousin,

Elizabeth Regina

MARY'S SECRET DIARY

She liked the petticoat! She was impressed by the stitching. I must make her more lovely things — maybe she will finally agree to see me.

Tell her that when one gets to our age, one should receive with both hands and give with one finger.

News from abroad

King Charles IX of France died in 1574. He was succeeded by the Duke of Anjou (the one who had not been grand enough for Mary) and the new king was no more interested in rescuing her than Charles had been.

Bothwell died in Denmark in 1578. He had been kept in such terrible conditions that he went mad. He died chained naked to a pillar and raving.

And in Scotland ... it was business as usual. In 1580 Sir James Balfour returned from exile to accuse the Earl of Morton of being involved in Darnley's murder. Morton was tried and found guilty. In 1581 he was executed with the machine he himself had designed – an early version of the guillotine called the Maiden.

By then Mary was more confined than ever. She'd had a bad fall from a horse, which left her with a damaged spine. Now she couldn't hunt, and to cap it all, she was very ill with gastric flu two years running.

News from abroad

In Scotland, it was business as usual! Like his granddad and his mum before him, the young King James VI was kidnapped by ambitious noblemen. James was 15, and had recently begun ruling for himself. He had fallen foul of his mum's old enemies, the Ruthven family, because as they saw it, he wasn't sufficiently Protestant.

James was their prisoner for ten months, till he managed to escape and make his way to St Andrews. For a while after that he was a bit more sympathetic towards his mum.

MARY'S SECRET DIARY

June 1583

...I think James is beginning to understand what I was up against. He is in touch with the Duke of Guise, to try and get me out of here. I have suggested to him that he and I might become joint-sovereigns. Have also asked him to execute Lindsay, for the unforgivable way he treated me, a crowned queen, at the battle of Carberry and afterwards. The brute deserves no less.

James didn't execute Lindsay, and he certainly wasn't planning to share his kingdom with his mum. But at last one of her powerful Guise uncles got involved with the Pope and Spain in the second big plot to spring Mary and restore the Catholic religion. It became known as the Throckmorton Plot after Sir Francis Throckmorton, brother of the English ambassador who had been so impressed with Mary when she was the young Queen of France.

Liz's loyal minister, Sir Francis Walsingham, who ran the best intelligence service in the world at the time, knew that Mary was in secret correspondence with the French ambassador. Here's part of the advice Mary had given the ambassador about writing to her...

...what I suggest is that you write in alum on very thin paper. If you soak it in a little water beforehand, the writing will be invisible, but when the paper is dipped in water again it will show white, and be clear enough to read. I am allowed to receive books, so you could also write between the lines, but use only every fourth page, and mark the book so that we know – I suggest a green thread. The high heels of slippers make an excellent hiding place for letters, and then of course there are the usual places, the backs of mirrors, or between the wood of coffers...

Throckmorton was caught and, after he'd been tortured, the whole plot was blown open. Elizabeth expelled the Spanish ambassador. And Sir Francis Walsingham decided that enough was enough. So long as Mary was alive she was trouble. She would always be the focus of Catholic plots. He decided it was time to get Mary.

THE FINAL PLOT

After the Throckmorton Plot, Mary was moved back to Tutbury, her least favourite prison. A new gaoler was put in charge: Sir Amyas Paulet, a fierce Puritan who hated Mary. The first thing he did was to rip down the precious state canopy which she kept over her chair all these years to remind herself and everyone else that she was a crowned queen.

MARY'S SECRET DIARY

January 1585

That ghastly man! He keeps such a sharp eye on me that there is not a chance of a secret letter getting through. I'm not even allowed ordinary letters. And Tutbury is as cold and smelly and uncomfortable as ever. I hate my life. I hate Paulet. I hate Liz.

This treatment went on for over a year. It was part of Walsingham's plan to cut off Mary completely from the outside word. Then, without explanation, on Christmas Eve 1586, she was moved to Chartley Manor, near Burton. And a few days later she took delivery of 23 secret letters!

MARY'S SECRET DIARY

16 January 1586

By the most amazing good fortune, the local brewer turns out to be a friend. He has made a slim waterproof pouch into which he puts letters, and then, before a delivery, he inserts the pouch through a tube in the bung of one of the beer barrels. My letters can leave the castle by the same route when the barrel is empty. It is wonderful, wonderful news! Despite all Liz's efforts, I can be in touch with the Spanish ambassador, the French, and anyone else I care to correspond with, and I can say anything I like for this route is completely safe...

The route was not safe, however, and the brewer was not a friend. What Mary didn't know was that Walsingham was behind everything. He had working for him a Catholic agent called Gilbert Gifford who had come to England to help Mary. Gifford had been captured by the English Intelligence service. Faced with the prospect of torture and a nasty death, he agreed to play along with Walsingham. He had visited the French embassy and told them that he could get letters to Mary. He had set up the beer barrel scam and bribed the brewer in Burton (who also took payment from Mary!). Now Gifford sat back and watched as every letter to or from Mary went via Walsingham.

WISE CHOICE, GIFFORD.

PRICKLY THISTLE FACT

Breaking the code
Mary wrote her letters in code. She used a mixture of Greek letters and numbers. But Walsingham had an ace code-breaker called Phelippes. He soon worked out what letters Mary's Greek letters and numbers stood for.

The Babington Plot

When she had first escaped to England, there had been so many rumours about the wicked Queen of Scots that most people thought twice about rescuing her. Now, 18 years on, she had become a romantic figure to many young Catholic Englishmen. A group of them were now hell-bent on helping her escape. Mary heard rumours about this plot and she made another disastrous decision. She wrote a letter.

To Sir Anthony Babington,
Somewhere near Wingfield,
Derbyshire.

25 June 1586

Dear Master Babington,
A little bird tells me that you are thinking of rescuing a certain lady in distress. Please tell me more.
Yours hopefully,
Mary, Queen of Scots.

Funny how that letter found its way to Babington, even though Mary didn't know his address. He wrote back enthusiastically.

1 July 1586

Your Majesty,
Such an honour to hear from you, I can't tell you how delighted I was to get your letter. You are absolutely right. Seven of us have sworn to kill the rival who usurped you

> *and keeps you prisoner. At the very same moment, I personally will come and release you. I long to kneel before you and kiss your royal hand,*
>   *Yours loyally,*
> *A. Babington*

Claude Nau, Mary's French secretary, warned Mary to be careful. Threats against the Queen's life were treason. Mary must take care not to give any sign that she was part of a plot to kill Elizabeth.

But Mary was worried that without foreign aid, the plot would fail and then where would she be? She brooded for three days, and then she made yet *another* daft decision. She wrote a long letter to Babington.

> *...all in all I fully endorse your plan, with the proviso that you must get some foreign backing. Suggest you contact the King of Spain, the King of France and the Duke of Guise. If you don't it will be curtains for all of us.*
>   *Your grateful queen,*
> *mary*

Babington, who was as stupid as Mary, decided to write and tell her! Not only that, he and his mates even posed

for a portrait. Walsingham rounded them all up in no time and on 4 August 1586 the bells of London rang out to celebrate the smashing of yet another plot against Queen Elizabeth. Mary, of course, knew nothing about this. There was no television or radio, so she only knew

what Paulet told her. And he told her only that she had been invited to a stag hunt with the local gentry, so she was looking forward to her first day out in a long time.

The stag hunt took place on 16 August. With Mary were Nau (her French secretary), Gilbert Curle (her Scottish secretary), Bastian Pages (who had organized masques for her all those years ago in Scotland), her doctor, her groom and her lady-in-waiting. Mary was still a good horsewoman, and she was ahead of the field when she saw that Sir Amyas Paulet was lagging at the back. She stopped to wait for him, and then saw a group of horsemen approaching.

MARY'S SECRET DIARY
17 August 1586

For one glorious moment, I thought it was Babington and his men come riding across the moor to rescue me and set me free. Instead it was vile Liz's men, come to accuse me of plotting against her life. I protested that I knew nothing about it, but their faces were hard, and they would have nothing but that I would go with them, alone. Now I am at some new place – Tixall, I think they said. My servants have been taken from me. I think they are going to kill me, quietly, and make out that I died in some accident.

People were certainly behaving as if she were dead already. Her personal things were gone through and pilfered. The money she had kept for paying her servants and for her own funeral was confiscated. She was moved to Fotheringay Castle. Mary's coachman was dismissed, as if to make it clear that she wouldn't be doing much travelling in future.

THE TUDOR TIMES

28 September 1586

SCOTS' QUEEN TO BE TRIED FOR TREASON

The Great Hall of Fotheringhay is being prepared for the state trial of the wicked Mary Queen of Scots. 'It's just been one plot after another against Queen Elizabeth, and this time we have proof that the Scots' Queen was plotting against our own queen's life,' said a source from the Palace of Westminster yesterday.

Mary's two secretaries, Claude Nau and Gilbert Curle, are known to have been helping agents of Sir Francis Walsingham with his inquiries. It is thought that they have confirmed as genuine letters which the Scottish Queen wrote to the traitor Anthony Babington.

When Mary was told she was going to be tried, she had quite a lot to say about it.

I am myself a queen, the daughter of a king, a stranger and the true kinswoman of the Queen of England. I came to England on my cousin's promise of assistance against my enemies and rebel subjects and was at once imprisoned. As an absolute queen I cannot submit to orders, nor can I submit to the laws of England without injury to myself, the King my son and all other sovereign princes.

Finally, however, she decided to appear in court. Cecil and Walsingham had just passed a new law, which said that if there were plots on her behalf, she was guilty whether she knew anything about them or not. So she knew there was absolutely no chance of her being found innocent. But, at least, she would get her first chance in 19 years to put her side of the case and get her voice heard in public.

> *Look to your consciences, and remember that the theatre of the world is wider than the realm of England.*

Mary did not get a fair trial. She was not trained in English law, she was allowed no lawyers, she was not allowed to see any of the incriminating evidence beforehand, and she was not even allowed to take notes. Yet she spoke so well on her own behalf that many of the councillors trying her ended up in tears.

It was the first time that many of these councillors had seen the Scottish queen, famous for her looks, charm and evil ways. They saw a woman who looked much older than her years – she was 43 at the time. She was overweight and lame. She wore a black satin dress with a white wimple. She was helped into court by her servants – her doctors, her ladies-in-waiting and Bastian Pages.

Mary's servants, her only supporters in court with her, were impressed.

…I wish you could have seen my lady facing her prosecutors without a sign of fear. She was so dignified and so quick-witted, for they came at her so fast with their accusations. Throughout they wished to speak only of her involvement in the Babington affair, but she took every opportunity to speak of how the English Queen has treated her. At the end of it all there was much noise and shouting, some calling that she be killed, but my lady remained quite calm, watching them all as if it were some pageant, and she a player along with the rest. Truly, she did well, but I think there is little hope. We must prepare ourselves for the worst.

THE TUDOR TIMES

26 October 1586

GUILTY OF TREASON!

The commission investigating the involvement of Mary Queen of Scots in the most recent plot against the Queen reached a guilty verdict yesterday. Immediately, both houses of Parliament voted to present a petition to Queen Elizabeth demanding her execution.

'Enough is enough. It's time she was removed from the scene,' said one MP.

But Queen Elizabeth may not sign the warrant for Mary's execution. She is known to dislike executions and, though the two women have never actually met, Mary is her cousin.

The last thing Liz wanted was to be responsible for executing Mary. She knew it would bring the wrath of every Catholic country in Europe down on her head – because more and more people were seeing Mary as a Catholic martyr. Then there was Scotland.

THE SCOTTISH HERALD

3 November 1586

FURY AT GUILTY VERDICT

Fury is spreading throughout Scotland at the decision of the English Parliament to ask for the execution of a Scottish queen. Commoners and nobles alike are outraged at the English assumption that they even have the right to try a Scottish monarch. When the King rode through the streets of Edinburgh he was booed for standing by and letting England condemn his mother.

'I mind her when she first arrived in Edinburgh,' said Mistress Annie Wishart. 'Aye, but she was bonnie. Spoke beautiful Scots, and smiled at everyone. The trouble started wi' the English, and it'll end wi' them. If she'd no marrit thon Darnley, none of this would have happened. I dinnae blame her for plotting against the English Queen. The English Queen had no right keepin' her in prison.'

Mary's son James had been none too bothered about his mother's trial. He wanted to keep in with Elizabeth, and anyway, he'd always been told what a bad woman his mum was. But as public opinion mounted in Scotland, he got nervous. If it was like this when she'd been found guilty, what would it be like when she was actually executed?

Guess ye in what strait my honour will be, this disaster being perfected, since before God I already scarce dare go abroad, for crying out of the whole people.

BOO!

SHAME!

The best solution, as far as Liz was concerned, would be for someone else quietly to take care of the problem for her... (You'd have thought that Elizabeth would have known better, considering what happened to Mary when *she* got someone to 'take care' of Dudley.) The idea was put to Sir Amyas Paulet, but Liz had chosen the wrong man. Paulet was far too upright. He loathed Mary, but he wasn't about to commit murder.

God forbid that I should make so foul a shipwreck of my conscience, or leave so great a blot on my poor posterity, to shed blood without law or warrant.

So Elizabeth just had to shoulder the blame herself. It took her months to get round to it. When she did, it was because her secretary managed to slip it in between a lot of other letters she was signing. Liz knew she was signing it, but she pretended she didn't, and she never forgave the secretary – Sir John Davison – who sent the warrant up to Fotheringhay immediately. The Earl of Shrewsbury arrived there on 7 February 1587 and told Mary she was to be beheaded the following morning.

JUST DOODLING...

MARY'S SECRET DIARY

8 Feb 1587

The day when I am to die.

The news was not exactly a surprise. I heard them hammering the scaffold weeks ago. Yet when the moment came, when George spoke the words, I must confess, I felt a shock. And he too, I could see, was upset.

I have done nothing but write letters these past few days. Have sent to Spain, saying that I disown James (he's been less than useless throughout, plus he's a Protestant) and that I leave my rights in the English crown to King Philip. Have sent the diamond Norfolk sent me to the Spanish ambassador, and left instructions that my servants be allowed to return to their own countries, and that my body be returned to France. I have made up gifts for all those I love, though God knows I have little enough left to give. I think I have thought of everything. Now I have one letter left to write – to King Henry in France. I have told him that my servants will tell him what really happened at my trial, and how I met my death. And emphasizing what I want the world to know – that I die because I am of the true faith. That has been my undoing from the moment I set foot in Scotland. That is why the Queen of England has feared and persecuted me. I die for the faith and I will wear red to prove it.

There was no sign of red as Mary entered the great hall of Fotheringhay Castle the next morning. She was dressed in black, with a white wimple as she had been at her trial. She had been up since 6 a.m. praying and saying goodbye to all her staff. At 9 a.m. the Sheriff of Nottingham came for her and found her kneeling in prayer.

201

ONLY WHEN FLETCHER SHUT UP DID SHE START TO PRAY IN ENGLISH – FOR THE POOR CATHOLICS WHO HAD TO LIVE IN ENGLAND.

PRAY PRAY PRAY

OOOOH! WHAT A FLAMING CHEEK!

THEN MARY'S WAITING-WOMEN, ELSPETH CURLE AND JANE KENNEDY, HELPED HER TO UNDRESS.

UNDERNEATH HER BLACK MANTLE AND OVERSKIRT SHE WAS WEARING RED – THE COLOUR OF ALL MARTYRS OF THE CATHOLIC CHURCH.

THEY TIED A WHITE CLOTH OVER HER EYES. THEN SHE LAID HER HEAD ON THE BLOCK.

IN MANUS TUAS, DOMINE, CONFIDE SPIRITUM MEUM

IT WAS A MESSY BUSINESS. THE FIRST BLOW DID NOT KILL HER. IT TOOK TWO MORE BLOWS TO CUT OFF HER HEAD.

CHOP! OOPS! CHOP! CHOP! CLUNK

FOR SEVERAL MINUTES AFTERWARDS HER LIPS SEEMED TO STILL BE MOVING...

IN TE DOMINO CONFIDO... Ouch that really hurt...

It wasn't just Mary's lips that moved. There were more shocks in store. First, the executioner picked up her head by the hair to show it to the 300 witnesses while he shouted 'God Save the Queen!' – but Mary's blood-streaked head rolled away from him across the floor, her hair grey and cropped very close to her skull. All he had left in his hands was her wig.

Then – more horror – the body seemed to move. Everyone gasped, thinking this woman refused to die. Then one of Mary's little dogs wriggled out from under her skirts. It ran over to Mary's head and sat beside it, howling. Mary Queen of Scots really was dead.

There was tight security at Fotheringhay. Mary's servants were all locked up out of harm's way. Then every single item of her clothing was burnt, and the hall scrubbed till there was not a sign of blood. The English authorities didn't want anyone collecting relics. The ports were sealed, which meant no ships could sail in or out and that Mary's last letters were held up for three weeks.

Elizabeth was terribly upset when the news was brought to her that Mary was dead. She blamed her secretary, saying that she only signed the death warrant 'in case' and that he should never have delivered it. (She put him in prison and fined him for doing his job.)

In France, when they heard the news, there were demonstrations in the streets. People wanted Mary made a saint by the Catholic Church.

In Scotland, James was glad his mum was out of the way (they'd never been close). But he ordered the court into mourning nevertheless. One of his earls was livid and showed up in armour, shouting, 'This is the proper mourning for the Queen of Scotland!'

And Philip of Spain was so furious with Elizabeth that he gathered a great Armada to invade England and take the crown which Mary had left to him. (Mary's death wasn't the only reason – Liz had been annoying him for years…)

Mary had asked to be buried in France, but her say counted even less than it had when she was alive. She was put in a lead coffin and left on a shelf in Fotheringhay Castle.

Not till five months later was a Protestant service held and her body buried at Peterborough Cathedral. No Scots were invited to the funeral.

When Elizabeth eventually died – 17 years later – Mary's son, James VI of Scots, became James I of England and united the two kingdoms under a single sovereign. Liz had known that Mary was her heir all the time, she just refused to come out and say so.

EPILOGUE

The pretty little princess who had led such a charmed life at the French court ended up with a pretty ghastly life over all. Beauty, energy and buckets of charm just weren't enough to succeed as a Catholic queen in a more or less ungovernable Protestant county. She had been Elizabeth's prisoner for 19 years, and, though she had been Queen of Scots since she was one week old, she had actually ruled Scotland for only six of her 45 years.

BUT LOOK WHAT A LOT I MANAGED TO PACK IN...

Men fell in love with her right up to the end, but she married the wrong ones and she escaped to the wrong country. She seemed to have a knack for always making the wrong decision.

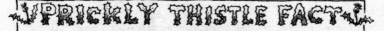

PRICKLY THISTLE FACT

Medical madness

There may be a medical reason for Mary's unwise behaviour. This century, someone discovered that she may have suffered from an illness called porphyria. It's an enzyme disorder and it can cause terrible stomach pains (and Mary had plenty of those) and also madness. One of Mary's descendants, George III, went completely bonkers with it. Other people just go in and out of irrational behaviour. So maybe at least some of Mary's peculiar decisions could have been because she was ill.

STRANGE DECISIONS? WHAT STRANGE DECISIONS?

It's interesting to compare Mary Queen of Scots with her cousin Liz. Liz fell in love with courtiers and suitors too, but she knew her power lay in keeping men guessing, and she never walked into the marriage trap. On the other hand, it was only by marrying that Mary produced an heir – and, even though he was a big disappointment to his mum, he did end up doing what everyone had always wanted to do: he ruled both England and Scotland.

We'll never know why Mary made so many mad decisions or chose such hopeless husbands. But people will no doubt go on being fascinated by her and try to make sense of her story, adding to all the thousands of poems, plays, novels and operas which have already been written about the dead glamorous and tragic Scottish Queen.